PRAISE FOR LAST ORDERS FIRST AND SECOND EDITIONS

"For guidance on making end of life provision, we particularly like the book *Last Orders*, by Patricia C Byron which has sections to fill in that guide you through leaving a Letter of Wishes detailing funeral arrangements and other concerns."

Good Housekeeping

"One of the intended consequences of *Last Orders* is to prompt the reader to discuss the issues raised and their wishes with their family and friends. I hope the author appreciates just how valuable this is at heading off potential post-death arguments and perhaps even avoiding costly litigation. The writer [of this review] would wholeheartedly recommend this book for both clients and practitioners alike."

The Law Society Gazette

"The detailed guidelines and checklists represent an indispensable aid to anyone who has to tackle the affairs of a loved one especially at a time of grief. For the executor, it will be a tremendous time-saving exercise"

The Society of Trust & Estate Practitioners Journal

"*Last Orders* is a very practical guide to death, and deals with all of the issues relating to all the aspects in your life that need to be addressed by your loved ones when you die. With its detailed guidelines and checklist [it] really is the perfect way to start the conversation… "

Manchester Law Society's Messenger

"..the modest cost will be one of your best investments.."

Archibald, Campbell & Harley, Edinburgh Solicitors.

"A splendid little book which steers a person through the essentials for the recording of information and expressing wishes, to friends and executors when the person dies."

Andrew Brooks LLM CTA TEP, Moxhay Advisory, London SW1.

"*Last Orders* is groundbreaking as it competently challenges the gap between what we think we know about what happens when someone dies and the reality. Sometimes complex, sometime simple, the process is far better served with forethought and direction. This book bridges the gap with empathy and all the practical guidelines and recommendations give help that no other books yet provide. Any experience that makes this tough process smoother is extremely welcome. After writing 30,000 wills over the last 20 years we know only too well how invaluable this guide is."

Stephen A. Oliver, Director of The Will Company, Northampton.

"Almost anyone will find this guide helpful in ensuring their explicit wishes after death are committed to paper...while family members or friends have lots of information and support."

Cancer Nursing Practice

PRAISE FOR LAST ORDERS FIRST AND SECOND EDITIONS

"'The book is aimed at the lay person so it is written in plain English. As legal practitioners, we can learn from Patricia's clear style and her hard work and research in providing practical questions which will result in useful answers in managing the estate of a deceased client.
…………………..its completion would make the executor's job easier.' -

Gill Steel, LawSkills Monthly Digest

"[It] is the only one not written by a lawyer. It is an excellent book and will make anyone – professional or client – have a long think about one of the most important things you have to do in life, namely die."

The Law Society Gazette's Top Ten books of 2019

"What a brilliant idea… I work in the funeral industry and so often, I meet families who are swamped and stressed with questions and indecision, not sure how to proceed because their dear departed loved-one left no instructions or preferences or information to help them, or they have spent inordinate amounts of time trying to sort through paperwork and belongings to try to find the information they need to take care of the estate. This is a remarkably simple but truly inspired book!"

M H Quayle, Funeral Celebrant

"This was recommended to me by a patient at the hospice where I work. It is essential reading for somebody who wants to get everything in place before saying their last goodbye."

Bernadette, Hospice Worker

"….an excellent book written from the heart and life experiences of being an executor. In today's ever increasing complex world we should all complete this book to help our loved ones with the heartache, arguments and anguish after our death. As a member of the Society of Will Writers and Will Writer myself I see so many families who suffer the loss of loved ones and have no idea what to do once they have passed away, this shouldn't be a taboo subject, families should talk about it and this book is the best guide to help them get their affairs in order. I would highly recommend this book to everyone, friends, family and clients."

A Shine, Will-Writer

"As a professional practising accountant for over 50 years, I am sorry that this work didn't come to hand much earlier. Apart from the peace of mind that users of this book can obtain, I would have really welcomed the opportunity to engage with clients on their long-term planning - financial and personal. This would have had allowed me to achieve two things. Firstly it would have enhanced the service I offered my clients and secondly it would have been the catalyst to meet each client regularly to review the directions they had previously given. Together, this would have been of great benefit to the clients.."

Michael C, Accountant.

LAST ORDERS

Your Executors' Guide to Your Letter of Wishes

SECOND EDITION

PATRICIA C. BYRON

STELLAR BOOKS

Published by:

Stellar Books
1 Birchdale
St Mary's Road
Bowdon
Cheshire
WA14 2PW

W: www.lastorders.org
E: info@stellarbooks.co.uk
T: 0161 928 8273

ISBN: 978-191-0275450

Second Edition (Paperback) Updated and revised in 2024.
Reprinted in 2025.

Also available:
Last Orders Second Edition (Hardback)
Published in 2019

Last Orders First Edition
Published in April 2010
Reprinted September 2010
Reprinted July 2012
Reprinted in August 2015

Last Orders is an Amazon Bestseller in several categories:
#1 in Law for the Lay Person
#1 in English Private, Property and Family Law
#1 in Death and Bereavement
#2 in Health, Family and Lifestyle
#2 in Mind. Body and Spirit
#22 in Books.

© Patricia C Byron 2024

The author asserts her moral right to be identified as the author of her work in accordance with the Copyright Designs and Patents Act 1988.

All rights reserved. No part of this publication may be reproduced, stored in any retrieval system, or transmitted in any form by any means, including electronic, mechanical, photocopying, recording or otherwise, without the prior written consent of the publisher.

Some names contained within the Foreword have been changed.

DISCLAIMER

Whilst every effort has been made to ensure that this book provides accurate information, it is impossible to predict all the circumstances in which it may be used. The author, publisher and retailer cannot be held liable to any person or entity with respect to any loss or damage caused by, or allegedly caused by, the information contained in this book.

To Absent Friends and Family

Cheers

CONTENTS

෧෬

FOREWORD viii

INTRODUCTION xi
    Leave a Good Legacy xi
    Why Make A Will?, DIY Will Kits xii
    Will Writers, Online Wills xiii
    Solicitors xiv
    Choosing Lay Executors xv
    Appointing a Professional Executor, Alternative Letters of Wishes xvi
    Frequently Asked Questions xvii

SECTION ONE - FIRST THINGS FIRST 1
    Your Immediate Checklist 1
    Useful Information for Your Executors 2
    Addresses & Employment 3
    Executors & Family: Registering a Death 4

SECTION TWO - CONTACTS 5
    The Address Book 5
    Mobile Phones, Email Accounts on Computers, iPads & Tablets 6
    Social Media Accounts 7
    Family & Friends Contact Form 8
    Other People to Contact Form 9
    Online & Social Media Form 10

SECTION THREE - FUNERALS 11
    Funerals: Religious, Civil, Humanist, No Funeral 13
    Let's Talk About ......Money Saving Funerals 25

SECTION FOUR - GRAVE THOUGHTS 28
    Natural, Woodland and Green Burial 30

SECTION FIVE - CREMATION	32
Cremation Fees	32
Direct Cremation, Disposing of Ashes	33
SECTION SIX - AFTER THOUGHTS	35
SECTION SEVEN – MEDICAL MATTERS	36
Advance Decisions / Living Wills	37
Advance Statement, Lasting Powers of Attorney	39
Health and Welfare LPA	40
Property and Financial Affairs LPA	41
Let's Talk About…… Organ Donation	42
Organ Donation	44
Leaving Your Body to Medical Science	45
SECTION EIGHT - WHERE THERE'S A WILL	47
SECTION NINE - MONEY MATTERS	51
Assets	51
Assets Form	53
Insurance Policies Form	54
Digital Assets, Online Accounts, Other Digital Assets	55
Income Streams	56
Online and Digital Assets Form	57
Loyalty Points, Liabilities & Loans	58
Liabilities & Loans Form	59
SECTION TEN - TAKING CARE OF BUSINESS	62
Business Form	67
SECTION ELEVEN - GOODS & CHATTELS	69
Goods & Chattels Form	75
SECTION TWELVE - CHILDREN	77
SECTION THIRTEEN - POOCH, PUSS & PETS	81
SECTION FOURTEEN - LAST ORDERS	86
USEFUL ADDRESSES	92
ACKNOWLEDGEMENTS	95

FOREWORD

"Why", I'm constantly asked. "Why would you write such a book?" Sadly, I can only answer it was because of the difficulties and trials I have had to face when tying up estates. Taking time to write *Last Orders* in the hope that it will shed light on a much-neglected subject seemed a small price to pay if it meant that others would not have to endure the same.

It all started when one of my closest friends, Maria, was diagnosed with cancer. She was a single lady, without children, had an elderly housebound parent and brothers she rarely saw. Her support network was her few close friends and I was one of her closest, with us having been friends for many years. We had cried together when she was diagnosed with breast cancer and I stayed close by her throughout her illness, from diagnosis, tests, scans, operations and the endless courses of chemotherapy she underwent, until the day she died, aged just 49.

She was a strong, vibrant lady, full of vitality and positivity; she firmly believed she would recover from the disease and never wished to contemplate the prospect of death. On just one occasion, a few weeks before she died, I attempted to open a conversation about her last wishes but it soon became clear to me that she did not wish to even consider such things, so my many questions went unanswered.

After four years of battling cancer, Maria passed away at home with just her close friends present. In spite of attempts to keep calm during those last days, I was in deep shock having never had to deal with a life-threatening illness at such close quarters. Within a couple of hours of her death, I was asked by the funeral director to search through her wardrobe to find an outfit so she could be dressed for her coffin. I felt distraught and helpless, rummaging through her most personal items at a time when I was, quite literally, grief-stricken. I chastised myself endlessly for not having done more to prepare for what was an inevitable outcome, or for not holding challenging conversations about what she wanted should the worst happen.

Despite the severity of her illness and prognosis, Maria left a Will so outdated that it bore no relation to the situation she was in. Nor were there any instructions for her funeral, so it replicated that of her father's, which had occurred just six months earlier. It bore none of her characteristic cheerfulness, nor was it a reflection of the vibrant globetrotter she had been. Later, when emptying her property, her belongings were distributed with some angst, contention and even confusion. To this day, I believe I could have and should have done more to help her address those difficult decisions which would have alleviated many of the problems which surfaced after her death.

A year before Maria died, a second friend, Kate, was also diagnosed with the same condition. As Kate's health started to fail, she asked me to be the executor of her Will. As fate would have it, I was simultaneously asked by three other people in as many months and, having experienced a death where no preparation had taken place, I was no longer cushioned by naivety. I now knew that the role of an executor – particularly of a single person's Will - brought with it overwhelming responsibilities.

Kate was also a single lady, without children, hugely bright with a wicked sense of humour. She, too, had no family she could call on and, although popular, was an intensely private individual. I knew it would be down to the executors to administer not just her estate after her death, but to cope with the final weeks of her life too. Once I realised the enormity of the task, I started to ponder on how I would not only cope, but handle matters appropriately when the time came. Taking care of an estate, the deceased's funeral, and disposing of their belongings is a daunting task for the most seasoned executor, even without the additional grief and loss of a close friend.

I was determined that I would not be left in the same state of regret as I had been after Maria's death. I needed to discover a way of discovering just what Kate's wishes were. The thought of having a conversation about such things was unimaginable. Nor did I want her to feel uncomfortable or pressurised during the making of those decisions. I wanted, instead, to give her the time which she would need to consider her choices. I had, what is called, a light-bulb moment: the idea of writing her a booklet, filled with questions that I needed answers to. That booklet was to become Kate's Letter of Wishes, the checklist I would use as my guide when the time came. Not only that, it was going to be my personal reminder and would not only clarify Kate's wishes but verify them too should anyone question my actions after the event.

I wrote the booklet as sensitively as I could, explaining why I was asking such difficult questions, and how it would help me arrange matters smoothly for her. I warned her before presenting her with a copy but, even then, it shocked her. Many tears were shed between us as she completed it, but it was important to me that she understood that I was only asking such difficult questions because I had been through similar issues with Maria, whom we both missed immensely. It was my desire, even my need, to do the right thing for her – including anything and everything surrounding her death, her funeral, the distribution of her belongings and, not least, her beloved chocolate Labrador, Coco. Fair play to Kate, once she understood my reasoning, she laughed with gusto and, with her black humour intact, entered into the spirit by answering my searching questions with some very colourful replies. During the last days of her life, at her bedside, she was still reading the notes I had made and we, together, tinkered with her funeral wishes.

When the dreadful time came, and Kate passed away peacefully at home, her requests were adhered to, to the letter. Her funeral was immensely moving, with Coco as chief mourner whimpering throughout the entire service. Many of the congregation said it was the best funeral they had ever been to which was gratifying because, despite very challenging circumstances, everything went without a single hitch. This was entirely down to Kate and her willingness to complete the book.

Feeling somewhat smug that Kate's funeral had been orchestrated with such ease, I mentioned my simple booklet to my mother, Kit, as I was also the executor of her Will. Kit, a larger-than-life vivacious lady, unfortunately, did not accept it with the same willingness as Kate, asserting that, as a family, we didn't need such a document. In fact, she did not wish to complete it at all so the book was forgotten and the files lay dormant on my computer.

When Kit died suddenly just one year later, the entire family was sent into shock. Feeling devastated at the loss of a deeply cherished mother is one thing but when the family sank into a stream of contentious fallouts, all of which could have easily been avoided had she completed my book, it brought grief to a whole new level. There were unrelenting disagreements about her funeral, her flowers, her gravestone, her belongings... the list was endless. To add fuel to the fire, whilst her Will addressed the distribution of her estate, complications arose which did nothing to calm very troubled waters within the family.

On reflection, I put much of the confrontation that arose down to family members' profound sorrow and an inability to handle the loss of our very precious Mum. Time and time again I wish I had been stronger when asking her to complete the book, which would have brought clarity to the confusion. Instead, even as executor, each step in administering her estate was excruciating, protracted and distressing for all concerned. I published *Last Orders* in 2010, in the hope that others will not have to endure the same.

All families are capable of falling out. For those who take the moral high ground and believe that they and their family are above such tribulations, I truly hope such optimism and tranquillity prevails. For the rest of us, who are unwilling even to risk such a thing, I remain hopeful that this book will help you and your family.

INTRODUCTION

This book is intended to assist anyone and everyone. It isn't a Will and shouldn't be considered or used as one. Whilst a Will centres on the deceased's assets, this book, which will serve as a Letter of Wishes, deals with the more personal, practical and intimate issues which executors and family members will have to address after a death. Once read, digested and completed, it should save an incalculable amount of stress and take most, if not all, of the guesswork out of administering an estate.

By completing *Last Orders*, you are taking the first steps to ensure you will leave behind what professionals call "a tidy estate". Coping with the death of a loved one is unquestionably one of life's most challenging events; making pivotal decisions at such a time, surrounding not just a funeral but events before and after it, can be tremendously stressful. By supplying your family and executors with answers to the practical questions in this book, you are eliminating confusion, offering clarity and relieving them of untold amounts of guesswork. And, when the time comes and the book is needed by your executors, you will be posthumously thanked endlessly for the foresight you had in completing it.

Leave a Good Legacy

We often talk about leaving a legacy, referring to a financial inheritance, but it is just as important to consider the wider implications of death. In the broader sense, a legacy also relates to how you will be remembered after death. We have all heard about shambolic estates which have taken years of heartache and vast expense to resolve. Worse still, families can be torn apart in the process. In that sense, a poor legacy lives on and can affect loved ones for the rest of their days.

But, by adopting some simple forward planning, you aren't just helping your nearest and dearest, you will almost certainly be on the way to avoiding family wrangles and surely, one of the greatest legacies anyone can leave behind is a family intact.

Why Make A Will?

Before addressing the contents of this book, it is important that you take the necessary steps, if you haven't already done so, of protecting your loved ones and your assets by making, (or if needs be, updating,) your Will. With today's complicated lifestyles, having a Will in place brings a level of certainty to how your estate will be distributed after your death. Who receives anything, and to what level they do, is down to the instructions and wishes documented in your Will.

If you die and have not made a Will, (or if, for whatever reason, your Will does not receive grant of probate), your estate will be distributed according to the law which may not correspond at any level with how you would have wished. Relying on the rules of intestacy (that is dying without a Will in place) to distribute your money can, at best, be seen as precarious, and at worst irresponsible.

Intestacy brings many difficult issues to the fore, and whilst this is not the book to explore all the complications that can arise, there are some myths to dispel. It may, for example, be worth noting that in England, without a Will in place, if you have children, the most your spouse can inherit from your estate is capped at £322,000 and thereafter, any remaining funds would have constraints placed upon them. So, for example, if you solely own a high-value property, your children could, potentially, end up owning the bulk of it, leaving your spouse in a very vulnerable position – particularly if your children are adults. Consider too, if you are separated but not yet divorced from your spouse and you suddenly die, your spouse, under the Rules of Intestacy could inherit significantly from your estate whilst a live-in partner of many years would have to jump through expensive legal hoops to make any kind of claim on your estate. So, unless you make provision for your live-in partner in your Will, they could be homeless as well as partner-less within a few weeks of your death. Think too about the financial implications of your estate being liable for Inheritance Tax which, with some legitimate and proper tax planning from a solicitor or Will writer, could be avoided altogether.

While there are a number of Will-making options available, getting around to making one is often a chore we delay and, whilst attending to it can present uneasiness, it may be useful to think of the task as not just an ordeal that has to be surmounted, but focus instead on the positive steps you are taking to care for your family and loved ones. Consider too the potential effects and ensuing consequences that a poorly drafted Will could have on your family, all at a time when you aren't there to assist them.

If you still need to make a Will, read on.

DIY Will Kits

Over-the-counter Will kits are a convenient option which offers an unrivalled immediacy to the Will-making process. They are, undoubtedly, the most inexpensive way of making a Will, retailing at around the ten pounds mark and available from most high street stationers. However, whilst they may suffice in the simplest of cases, for those who have estates of significant value with convoluted assets or a complex family structure – (also known as a 'blended' family), they are largely unsuitable.

There is a huge capacity for errors and, if the DIY Will is completed incorrectly, a sorry mess can ensue leaving part or all of the Will invalid. The Society of Trust and Estate Practitioners, (STEP), a worldwide professional body which oversees trusts, estates and legacies, has collated many examples where the results have been "disastrous". The repercussions for a family can be immense. Even if a Will has been completed correctly, is legally sound and sails through probate, it may not have been drafted with tax efficiency in mind and could negate any meagre saving that was made in purchasing the kit in the first place. Equally problematic, it may have been written in such a way that proves to be particularly difficult for lay executors to administer.

Will Writers

Will writers aim to take the stress out of making a Will by offering convenience at an affordable price. The service offered is usually seen as an inexpensive alternative to law firms. Some are sole traders, others are sizeable firms, some are legally qualified, some not. Usually, they visit potential clients in their homes, ensuring the process is effortless and hassle-free.

Unfortunately, as Will writing is an unregulated profession, anyone can set up a website and call themselves a 'Will writer' without the necessary qualifications, training or insurance which would assure redress if a Will has been incorrectly drafted. So, if you elect to use a Will-writer, it makes sense to ensure that you choose one who is either a member of the Society of Will Writers (SWW) or the Institute of Professional Will-writers (IPW), both of which ensure their members are trained and have professional indemnity insurance.

As with most things in life, there are good and bad in all things and that includes Will-writers. It is wrong to say that all should be sidestepped. There are very reputable Will-writing firms that provide a valuable service to their clients, but it is widely acknowledged that the lack of regulation is unsatisfactory and, although they may well produce fodder for investigative journalism, it equally casts a slur on trustworthy and proficient firms which offer a tremendously valuable service.

Online Wills

Unless your Will is simple, your family structure uncomplicated and your estate modest, avoid. Sadly, and crucially, errors which are made in any Will making process are usually only discovered after death, once the application for probate has been made, by which time it is too late. In such circumstances, the Will could then be deemed useless and the intestacy rules would decide how your estate would be distributed.

If you have doubts as to whether your existing Will has been correctly drafted, it is strongly recommended that you get it checked by a solicitor or a member of STEP whilst you have the ability to rectify any mistakes which could prove problematic for your loved ones in the future.

Solicitors

Solicitors offer a professional, water-tight Will which should leave nothing to chance. They are legally qualified, robustly regulated and, most importantly, covered by insurance for the rare occasion when some form of recompense is required.

If you wish to adopt a more belt and braces approach, you may wish to seek out a solicitor with STEP qualifications. As previously mentioned, Will-writing is an unregulated profession and while solicitors are regulated by the Solicitors Regulation Authority, that in itself doesn't guarantee Will-writing proficiency. Solicitors who have taken additional STEP courses and examinations, specifically in Will-writing and estate planning, will have TEP after their names and will almost certainly offer a more thorough service.

In 2013, the Law Society launched its own accreditation scheme: the Will & Inheritance Quality Scheme Accreditation (WIQS). Its protocol recommends that solicitors advise Will-making clients on the importance of not just the legal aspects of making a Will, but also the wider implications of neglecting practical issues such as funeral arrangements (11.2), organ donation (11.2.1), maintaining a personal assets log (2.6) and care of one's pet (10.6). If you have made a Will with a solicitor recently, they will have hopefully drawn your attention to these matters. If not, *Last Orders* will fulfil the brief for you.

Clearly, instructing a solicitor to make your Will is likely to be the most expensive option, but it could and should ultimately save your beneficiaries time – inasmuch as the Will should receive probate without any difficulty, money – if your solicitor has advised you on Inheritance Tax - and most importantly, should relieve your family of an inordinate amount of stress from the chaos that can ensue from some of the other Will-making options.

Obviously, the complexity and size of your estate will, more than likely, determine which Will-making avenue you choose. Someone with three ex-wives in tow, and children scattered liberally throughout the country will have different priorities and needs to a single, childless person, and the cost of tailoring one's Will to encompass such differences will vary accordingly. Whichever option you choose, it is important that you review your Will from time to time to ensure that its content is still relevant. It is recommended that this is done around every five years, or if your circumstances change.

Choosing Lay Executors

When you make a Will you will need to choose executors, over the age of 18, who will carry out your wishes and administer your estate. Most people choose to appoint two people although up to four is permissible – one or two can remain in reserve should the originals, for whatever reason, be unavailable. Any or all of them may or may not be beneficiaries. If you made your Will some time ago, you may wish to review the suitability of those you have chosen. They may have been suitable candidates to take on the role then but are they now? Are they still physically and mentally fit or even alive?

It is important that you choose wisely: the executors of your Will should be people whom you trust implicitly, are morally sound and, ideally, relatively familiar with your affairs. They should have the time, the skills and the wherewithal to deal with the myriad problems which can arise and, of course, be willing to take on the role. Equally important, and rarely commented upon, is the need for your executors to have some kind of rapport; there is little to be gained in appointing people who find it impossible to agree on anything; a meeting of minds is often crucial.

If you wish to appoint non-professional executors such as family members, you will need to weigh up whether your family would be able to withstand any tensions that may arise. Your children may have always had a harmonious relationship, but would it survive the additional pressures of a contentious house sale? Grieving for the loss of a loved one and making pivotal, irreversible decisions are not happy bedfellows and, whilst saving money in executors' fees is one thing, leaving a family intact is something else entirely. Appointing a professional executor could be the answer.

A lay executor's lot can be particularly arduous and challenging. In return, there is no salary, but expenses are usually paid out of the estate upon production of relevant receipts. While your executors will undoubtedly save your estate a tidy sum in solicitors' fees, you will need to play your part too by helping them by completing this book. If you are making or re-making your Will, you may wish to reward your executors by leaving them something extra for their work.

With the internet playing a pivotal role today in providing necessary material via governmental websites, money-saving forums and charities' websites, (www.ageuk.org.uk for example), and, if your Will and estate are simple enough, there is sufficient excellent information available for any lay executor to apply for probate themselves without involving professionals. Should they run into difficulty they can always revert to appointing a solicitor.

Appointing a Professional Executor

You may wish to appoint a professional in the shape of a solicitor, bank or Will-writer to act as your executor and there are sound reasons for doing so. They should have the ability to offer unbiased, objective advice and bring a level of expertise to the administration of an estate. This can be advantageous if your Will is particularly complex, contentious or overstretches the skills of a non-professional executor. Similarly, they will be highly experienced in liquidating estates and should know all the procedures to recoup any monies which are owed to the estate – not least from the taxman. Finally, and importantly, if you appoint a professional, they will release any non-professional executor from being liable for any mistakes which could be made during the course of settling the estate.

There are firms which offer competitive fixed fees for the work involved but some can prove costly so, if you are about to make your Will and appoint a professional (or, even if you have already appointed one) enquire as to what their probate fees are likely to amount to based on the value of your estate as it stands today. It will be useful information for your family and could offer you the opportunity to change your executors if the fees are extortionate.

Some solicitors may lack the 'personal touch' detailed in the following pages, so it is important that you familiarise them with the more practical aspects of your life. Complete this book and ensure that your professional executor knows where to find it. They may wish to store it for you.

Alternative Letters of Wishes

While reading this book you will come across references to technology and the revolutionary effect that it has had on our lives. Storing one's Letter of Wishes is no different. There are websites, apps and online storage facilities, (clouds), where you can store almost every detail of your life, your bank accounts, assets, passwords, as well as your Letter of Wishes. Not all are suitable, some are misleading and most are expensive. Just be mindful that storing all your life details and last wishes in several different places may produce conflicting information and could confuse matters for your executors.

To what degree you wish to embrace this kind of technology is entirely down to how comfortable you are with not just the usage, but also the security, of that technology. Just as some people will not entertain online banking, choosing to store the details of your life in a cloud is entirely a personal decision.

We also need to bear in mind that we are very much at the mercy of trends and clouds, potentially, are no different. Years ago it may have been useful to store details and documents on floppy discs or CD-ROMs, both of which aren't just obsolete, but impossible to use with current computers. Today we are using memory sticks and very useful they are too, but already, many of the newer devices sold do not have the capacity to use them.

There are other, simple ways of videoing or voice recording yourself on tablets, smartphones and iPads should you wish to say a few words to your loved ones after you have reached the pearly gates.

If, like me, you are not afraid to embrace technology but, in certain instances, simply prefer pen and paper, there's good reason: it is tangible and traceable. It can be referred to without special equipment and, being a precious document, which will be used, referred to and cherished long after death, it persuades me that sometimes, simplest is best.

You can, of course, write your own Letter of Wishes on an A4 piece of paper. But, a note of caution: I have heard on countless occasions from people who, on emptying a deceased's property, have found stray pieces of paper containing the deceased's last wishes long after the funeral has taken place and possessions have been distributed, which is beyond sad.

Frequently Asked Questions

What is the difference between a Will and a Letter of Wishes?

Leaving a tidy estate generally revolves around two things: making a Will, and writing a Letter of Wishes.

We all know that a Will is a legal document which determines how your estate will be distributed. A Letter of Wishes, by contrast, is a non-binding, non-legal document, written to guide executors about specific things that should happen after death. Whilst this sometimes refers to the management of trusts and the appointment of professional advisors, it is just as likely to refer to the wider issues detailed in this book which accompany the end of life, such as funeral arrangements, preference for burial or cremation and the distribution of belongings.

Do executors have to follow this Letter of Wishes?

Executors have the right to overrule any requests laid out in this book. However, they will, hopefully, be happy to honour and feel morally obliged, to follow these *Last Orders* as far as practically possible. It's important that you help them too by ensuring your wishes are reasonable, realistic and achievable, giving them every opportunity to fulfil them.

It is well-recognised that adhering to a loved one's wishes after a death goes a long way towards healing and the acceptance of loss. If you are an executor reading this, it may be worth considering what effect ignoring the deceased's wishes will have on you and your future relationship with the bereaved before you consider ignoring them.

If executors can ignore a Letter of Wishes, why bother writing one?

Indeed, but if your executors are likely to ignore your wishes, why appoint those particular executors in the first instance? If you have doubts as to whether your wishes will be adhered to, consider changing your executors. Consult with your solicitor or Will-writer.

How often should I review my *Last Orders*?

As with a Will, it is important to review the content of this book periodically to ensure that it still represents your wishes. There are pages contained within which have intentionally been left blank for any additional information you may wish to supply. There are other pages which have forms to complete.

- Forms in Section 9, relating to your finances, bank accounts and insurance policies, should be photocopied and used as templates for annual updates.
- Keep them in a safety deposit box, a home safe or somewhere secure within your home.

How safe is it to store these details in one document?

There are valid security issues to consider. You can complete as much or as little of the book as you feel comfortable with. What is key, particularly in the case of bank accounts, policies and credit cards, is that your executors know of their existence.

Where passwords are required you may wish to store them separately in a safe or document box.

Access to any online accounts – even social media, has its own security issues; online hackers and even, potentially, the computer geek at the local computer repair shop all carry potential dangers so a book such as this poses fewer risks than first considered.

Where should I keep my *Last Orders*?

Digesting and completing this book will take time. You will, quite possibly, wish to revisit and change your mind about answers you have given so until you are fully satisfied that you have completed your wishes, advise your executors of its whereabouts.

My preferred storage option is to use a safe within your home; they aren't expensive to purchase and it will offer you immediate access to the book as and when you require it. Or, buy a document box and store it in the most secure location within your home. They are perfect for keeping all manner of documentation and small keepsakes in, which will offer invaluable assistance for your executors. Hunting for vital documents in the early days after a death is extremely stressful. Ease your family of that burden by gathering and placing them altogether within the box.

If you are appointing professional executors such as a solicitor or Will-writer, they will almost certainly store it for you.

How to complete this book

There are many different topics in the following pages, on a wide variety of subjects. Some observations and questions have been specifically included in an attempt to encourage you to think about issues which you may, up until now, have avoided or not considered. Indeed, one of the book's chief aims is to prompt you into seeking specialist advice in any area you feel is relevant to you. This book, no matter how well-intentioned, cannot address all the issues in depth, nor consider all the variables of every individual's life.

You will encounter some thought-provoking questions which require answers. Wherever there is a question mark followed by a grey box, complete it as necessary. It is advisable to use an ink or ballpoint pen, using block capital handwriting, and sign and date your *Last Orders* in Section 14. Should you change your mind about an answer - and we all do - cross out the old answer and write in the new and then date it. Let your executors see your train of thought; it may prove useful.

Not all sections will be applicable to you so consider the ones which are relevant as standalone exercises and complete them one at a time. Some will need time to reflect, others will be very simple and straightforward. As for those sections which are irrelevant to you, they may contain useful information which you can pass on to others.

You can complete as much or as little of the book as you wish and it need not be done in one sitting. The choices you make will, in themselves, demonstrate to your executors the issues which are important to you. For example, you may not wish to answer questions about certain aspects of your funeral but may merely wish to state your preference for the music which is to be played. Or you may wish to let it be known for example, in the Goods and Chattels section, that the picture that is currently above the fireplace with the tatty frame was actually painted by great-uncle Rupert, that Dorothy at number 23 has a spare set of keys to your house and that, in the Pets section, your cat is allergic to chicken.

In answering any of the questions, bear in mind that it is not sufficient to say that a partner knows this or X knows that. Consideration should be given to the emotional state that your partner or X may be in. Additionally, there must be ample information in case a situation arises where neither your partner nor X is available.

And finally…..it's good to talk

Most family fall-outs that occur after a death are due to a lack of understanding of the deceased's wishes, so before you start completing this book it is strongly recommended that you take the time to hold a conversation with your family and the executors of your Will about the topics raised. It need not be a morbid or difficult conversation; it is the responsible thing to do.

Once broached, most family members welcome the opportunity to clarify, explain and put minds at ease. With the conversation opened, all manner of concerns and worries can be discussed; airing opinions will only make matters simpler in the long run. You can explain your funeral choices and ask for your family's opinion. Align, if possible, your wishes with theirs. Ask whether anyone has any particular requests regarding family keepsakes or items within your home. Determine whether anyone wants your pet. Discuss the possibilities of organ donation. Ask them what their concerns are. Tell them about this book and, if it helps, use it as a discussion tool. It is applicable to everyone, regardless of age.

And remember, just because you are completing your *Last Orders,* there are no guarantees that all of your family members will outlive you; a discussion may encourage them to address their own *Last Orders* too.

SECTION ONE

First Things First

Before you start completing your *Last Orders* it is essential that your family and executors are equipped with the following crucial tools to assist you. Pass on these details as soon as possible:

- ➢ A set of keys to your property. ☐
- ➢ The alarm code to your property. ☐
- ➢ The access code to any safe you have. ☐
- ➢ The access code(s) or password(s) to your computer(s). ☐
- ➢ The location of your Will. ☐
- ➢ The location of your *Last Orders*. ☐
- ➢ Advise your executors whether you wish to donate your organs. ☐

Useful Information for Your Executors

Your full name: _____

Your maiden name: _____

Your full postal address: _____
_____

Your date and place of birth: _____

The location of your birth certificate:* _____

Your National Insurance number:* _____

Location of your marriage/civil partnership/divorce certificate(s):* _____
_____

Your (or your spouse's) occupation: _____

Details of any benefits or pensions you are receiving from the government:* _____
_____

Location of your passports: _____

Your car's registration number and log book*: _____

Location of driving license: _____

*Place in document box

Addresses & Employment

It would be useful for your executors to have some additional background information. This could assist them to write a eulogy, search for lost pensions, bank accounts or could even help find your Will if it is misplaced.

Have you ever been known
by any other name? _____

Previous address: _____

Period you lived there: _____

Address prior to that: _____

Period you lived there: _____

★ ★ ★

Current Employer: _____

Period you worked there: _____

Previous Employer: _____

Period you worked there: _____

Previous Employer: _____

Period you worked there: _____

Executors & Family: Registering a Death

- The first step in registering a death is to obtain a Medical Certificate of Cause of Death which has been signed by either the GP who had been treating the deceased, or, if the death occurred in hospital, a hospital doctor.

- In England, Wales and Northern Ireland, the death must be registered with the Registrar in the location where the death occurred within 5 days, (8 in Scotland) from the date of death. This includes Bank Holidays and weekends unless the death has been referred to a coroner.

- You will need to make an appointment with the nearest Registrar. In some instances, when the death occurs in a hospital, it automatically informs the local Registrar and an appointment is made on your behalf.
Visit www.gov.uk/register-offices and type in your postcode.
Alternatively, call your local council which will be able to direct you accordingly.

- The person registering the death can be:
    - A close relative.
    - A person who was present at the time of death.
    - The person who is arranging the funeral (but not the funeral director).
    - An executor of the estate.
    - The governor, matron or chief officer of a public building where the death occurred.
    - A person living in, and responsible for, a house, lodgings or apartments where the death occurred.

- They will need to produce information about the deceased, most of which can be found on page 2.
    - The date and place of birth.
    - The date and place of death.
    - Ideally, the deceased's birth certificate or passport.
    - The occupation and marital status of the deceased.
    - If the deceased was married or a widow, the name and occupation of the spouse.
    - Proof of the full address of the deceased; a utility bill or bank statement will suffice.
    - Details of any pension or government benefits the deceased was claiming.

- The Registrar will provide two certificates: a Certificate of Burial or Cremation (the 'green form'), which will be required by the undertaker for an application for cremation, which will need to be completed. You will also receive a Certificate of Registration of Death for completion if the deceased was in receipt of a state pension or benefits.

- It is advisable to obtain extra copies of the death certificate, particularly if the estate is complex. Each insurance company, bank, financial body and social media platform will require sight of an original copy for their records before further action can take place and it may take time for them to return originals. There is an additional charge of between £8-£12 (2024) for extra copies but having them can expedite matters considerably.

SECTION TWO

Contacts

One of the first tasks an executor will have to carry out is to inform friends, family and colleagues of your passing. If one considers that this is likely to take place soon after they themselves have heard the news, when they are likely to be in a state of shock, just knowing whom to contact can be tremendously useful. Today, our friends and family are more widespread than ever and, for the executor, the task of uncovering their whereabouts, is increasingly challenging. They will have to find, access and check records in your address book, your mobile phone and any computers you have.

The Address Book

Finding an old address book may, at first, appear to be useful, but how current and important are the names? The ordeal of contacting strangers, to advise them of the death of someone they have not seen or heard from in 20 years is upsetting for all concerned. So, the first thing you can do to assist is to supply a list of the people you wish to have notified. It need not be extensive - perhaps one or two per group of friends who can, in turn, relate the news to others. Alternatively, you may choose to leave an existing address book with the names and contact details of those who should be informed, highlighted with a marker pen. If so, where do you keep your address book and how will you mark the people to contact?

> *Consider keeping your Christmas card list or the list of attendees of any annual reunion. This will show those with whom you are in touch, even if it is only on an occasional basis. If there is such a list, where do you keep it?*
>
> *Or, find last year's list and place it in your document box.*

Mobile Phones

In order to establish who your regular contacts were, your executors and family will also need to access your contact list from your mobile phone and, if necessary, retrieve text and phone call records. This will also potentially, enable them to download photographs or videos you have taken. Problems can arise when a smartphone requires a password or code in order to access these details and, if this applies to yours, you may wish to pass on those details now. In any event, it is useful for someone, somewhere to know family members' passwords for worst case scenarios. For mobiles (and other gadgets) which use fingerprint, face or iris recognition as a means of access, ensure that a password is set up as an alternative method of access.

Your Mobile Phone Password is where?

Your Voicemail Access Code is where?

➢ Consider periodically tidying up the content of your mobile phone, deleting unwanted photographs and names of those people who aren't part of your circle of contacts. It all helps.

Email Accounts on Computers, iPads & Tablets

Other sources for contacts which need to be checked are computers, tablets and/or iPads. While it appears to be simple enough for those with just one device with a single email account, many of us have multiple gadgets which hold some email accounts but not others.

All devices will need to be accessed by your executors to retrieve, amongst other things, your email address book, your accounts and any invoices that may arrive via email.

Either write the passwords below or, should you prefer, keep them in a safe place and advise your executors where to find them. It is important that you do not place passwords in your Will.

Computer Password is where?

IPad Password is where?

Tablet Password is where?

Social Media Accounts

Social media platforms, such as Facebook, Instagram, X and online chat forums are commonly used as a means of communicating with friends, family and online acquaintances and should also be considered as an important area which should be checked for contacts. For many of us, such platforms can hold a vast amount of information about our lives, cataloguing our milestones, interests and friendships; they can also hold personal photographs or videos that may be of immense sentimental value to family and friends after a death. If your account(s) hold such personal memorabilia, a worthwhile habit to get into (regardless of age), is to download the images onto your computer and share them with loved ones now.

You will need to consider what you want to happen to these social media accounts after you die. Most platforms' licenses expire when the account holder dies; the account will need to be closed.

It is an area which is becoming increasingly complex and executors (or someone they elect) will need to familiarise themselves with the various platforms, each having its own unique terms and measures which will need to be adopted. You may wish periodically to give your online presence a spring clean by deleting social media platforms or forum memberships that are no longer used.

On the next three pages, there are three Contact Forms to complete.
- On Page 8, write down the names of those whom you wish to be contacted. Include family members - even if they are estranged. Elaborate too, in what capacity you know non-family members – for example, colleague, neighbour, the golf club, U3A, church and so on.
- On Page 9, write down the names of professionals you use.
- On Page 10, your online presence. Consider how you wish to pass on your passwords.
- For more on your digital footprint, visit the section on Money Matters on page 55.

Facebook, the largest social media platform, has 3 billion active users worldwide. If you have an account, you can nominate someone to manage your page after your death. Log into your Facebook account and go to Settings, then Manage Account and finally Legacy Contact. Input the name of the person you wish to manage the account. Advise your chosen custodian of your password. Alternatively, on the same page, you can request to have your account permanently deleted after death.

A memorial page can be set up for friends and family to keep in touch. Your chosen custodian will be able to respond to friend requests, pin a tribute post and more. Do you wish this to happen?

Who should set it up?

Other social media accounts can be deactivated simply by logging on to the account's settings. In order to download data, such as images and videos, your executors will require permission from the social media platform.

FAMILY & FRIENDS CONTACTS	TELEPHONE NUMBER or EMAIL ADDRESS	RELATIONSHIP or CONNECTION

OTHER PEOPLE TO CONTACT	TELEPHONE NUMBER	EMAIL ADDRESS
Doctor		
Dentist		
Employer		
Cleaner/Home Help		
Gardener		
Alarm Provider		
Home Security Service		
Religious Clergy Member		
Solicitor		
Accountant		
Stockbroker		

ONLINE AND SOCIAL MEDIA ACCOUNTS	LOG IN USERNAME OR EMAIL ADDRESS	ON WHICH DEVICE?	CLOSE (C), MEMORIALISE (M), OR DEACTIVATE (D)	PASSWORD PASSED ON TO EXECUTORS?
Email Account (1)				
Email Account (2)				
Facebook				
X (1)				
Instagram				
Chat Forums				
LinkedIn				

SECTION THREE

Funerals

The cornerstone of any funeral will almost certainly depend on the religious beliefs you hold and whether you wish to adhere to its funeral ceremony. In religious parlance, a funeral is the deceased's commendation to God and, for those of faith, there are prescribed rituals that are followed which simplifies the decision-making process. For those who are agnostic or atheist, and have a more fluid or non-existent relationship with religion, there is more to consider. In any event, whether you are a fervent believer, an agnostic or a committed atheist, before you choose the elements of your funeral, it is important to recognise that, for loved ones, the service can be a source of comfort, offering a sense of closure. So, while it is important to outline your own personal funeral choice – and that, in itself, is a commendable and generous thing to do - it is worth considering the effects your preferences will have on your nearest and dearest.

The funeral industry in the UK is in a state of transition. In recent years there has been a move away from traditional, sombre funerals which were seen by some as being overly rigid and formulaic. Instead, we as a nation appear to be increasingly moving towards a more improvised, celebratory approach which can offer a personalised event and gives greater opportunity for freedom of expression. Touches of humour injected by family and friends are now welcomed, relieving tension and creating a more relaxed atmosphere.

For consumers, there is a bewildering array of options to make any funeral as striking or simple as you want it to be; almost any choice, no matter how seemingly wacky, is acceptable. From themed, colour co-ordinated affairs to undertakers in Victoriana garb, from the hire of a single hearse to horse-drawn carriages; floral tributes from a single rose to six feet long wreaths; coffins can be made of green eco-friendly cardboard, wool, rattan, or banana leaves. We can be buried in woodland pastures or commission a boat trip specifically for ash-scattering, our ashes can explode in colourful firework displays or sit on a mantelpiece in a paperweight. There's a vast catalogue available to make any funeral and its aftermath an intensely personal and unique occasion. Conversely, the variety of options can create disagreements amongst grieving families if wishes haven't been expressed. It is important, therefore, that you assess the merits of the many offerings so that you can create a tone which suits you and, importantly, avoids potential disagreements within your family.

Funerals can be costly. They needn't be. There are ranges for every pocket and size, and funeral directors usually offer different levels of service (such as silver, gold and platinum) and prices vary accordingly. According to a Sun Life report, location is also relevant too with prices ranging from £5,283 in London to £3,317 in Northern Ireland for an average funeral. It is up to you to determine just how much you choose to spend, after all the cost will, most likely, be paid for out of your estate. Regardless of which funeral director you choose to use, be aware they have little control over disbursements such as burial plot prices and cremation costs.

If you do not wish to choose the various elements of your funeral, later in this section you can elect someone to decide on your behalf. A word of warning: whilst leaving family members to make key decisions may appear convenient, it is not without its pitfalls. Many of us handle loss badly. When grieving, we often go into a state of shock, make poor decisions and even poorer choices. Families with a history of simmering tensions, and even those who have had harmonious relationships during a parent's lifetime can suddenly, without that central parental figure, fall into disputes over the most trivial things: religious content, style, timing and costs to name a few. Sadly, it is a familiar story and one that's regularly heard within funeral directors' and solicitors' offices.

Legally speaking, executors are responsible for ensuring that the deceased's funeral wishes are implemented. They are also responsible for the cost of your funeral if it outstrips the value of your estate. If you wish them to adhere to your *Last Orders,* keep your wishes achievable. It would defeat all good intentions if the choices you make are unrealistic. Your executors and family will undoubtedly want to do their best for you. Make it easy for them to do just that.

Consider, first of all, the basis of your funeral and tick which you would prefer:

Religious

Each religion has its own special way of conducting funerals. Christians, for example, have an array of hymns and prayers to choose from. Muslims, Jews, Hindus and Buddhists have time-honoured, defined rituals which are usually adhered to and therefore, by definition, there are fewer decisions to make.

I would like a religious funeral. I am of the _____ **faith.** ☐

Civil Funeral Service

A Civil Funeral Service is a dignified ceremony which reflects the beliefs and values of the deceased. Although it is predominantly non-religious, there is the option to include prayers and hymns. This lends itself to a collective contribution from the congregation in song and/or prayer, the benefits of which, for mourners, shouldn't be underestimated. The service is often highly personalised, with family members and friends taking an active role via readings, poetry and songs which reflect the deceased's life. Although anyone can conduct such a ceremony, there are Civil Funeral Service celebrants who are trained and skilled in such matters. It can take place almost anywhere other than a religious building.

I would like a Civil Funeral Service ☐

Humanist

Humanists have no religious beliefs and see life and death through a sense of logic, reason and evidence. The funeral is usually conducted by a Humanist celebrant who will tailor a unique ceremony based on the deceased's life and their loved ones' wishes. Family and friends can also contribute to the proceedings. There is no religious or spiritual content permitted, that is, no prayers, hymns or blessings. The ceremony can be held anywhere other than a religious building, although they are often held in crematoria, cemeteries or burial sites.

I would like a Humanist Ceremony ☐

No Funeral

Although some kind of service, no matter how austere, may offer comfort and closure for mourners, you may not wish to have a funeral at all; that is no service, no cars, no flowers, low costs.

I do not wish to have a funeral. ☐

If this is the case, go straight to page 29 for burial or page 32 for cremation.

When completing the following questions, remember that it is important that as well expressing what you do want, state too anything that you do *not* want to include in your funeral.

1. Have you chosen or considered which funeral director you wish to use?
   If so, supply details of name, address and telephone number:

2. If you are finding it difficult to arrange your funeral, please specify who should choose on your behalf? Consider your spouse, children, siblings, parents.

3. The cost of your funeral will (most likely) come out of your estate. If choices have to be made on your behalf, on a scale of 1 to 10, with 1 being the least expensive and 10 the most expensive, how much do you wish to spend?

4. Or, do you already have you a funeral plan in place? If so, where is the documentation for it? Place the paperwork within your document box.

5. Do you wish to be embalmed?

6. Do you permanently wear any item(s) of jewellery?

> ℬ❄ℭ
>
> *Embalming is purely for cosmetic effect and, should you prefer for your remains not to be viewed, there is little to be gained in paying for the process. The procedure should be optional and, if it is not required, it is important that your executors advise the funeral director accordingly.*
>
> *Also, note that should you wish to be buried at sea or in a natural burial ground, embalmment is prohibited. Conversely, if you are donating your body to medical science it is compulsory.*
>
> ℬ❄ℭ

7. If so, would you wish this/these item(s) to be buried with you? Or have you bequeathed these items to individuals in your Will? Please specify which item(s) and to whom:

8. Do you have any preference as to the design of the coffin?

9. Or, have you gone down the wholesaler route and purchased a coffin? If so, where is it and who knows about it?

10. Have you considered whether you would like any items to be placed alongside you in the coffin? Please list:

11. Have you any preference as to the clothes you would like wear in your coffin? Some ladies may wish to wear a favourite dress, gents their favourite college, military or cricket club tie, others wear pyjamas and bed socks. If all else fails, funeral directors can, at a cost, supply gowns or shrouds.

It is customary to place mementos in the coffin which can be of sentimental value or intensely personal. The range of favoured items is huge: money, food, sweets, letters to the deceased are all popular.

Frank Sinatra's assortment of items for his coffin included bourbon, cigarettes and a bunch of dimes to call home. Today's equivalent is the mobile phone, which is one of the UK's most requested items.

Roald Dahl had chocolates, pencils and his snooker cues. Elizabeth Taylor had Richard Burton's love letters; J F Kennedy had a 9 ½ inch whale's tooth which had been given to him by wife Jackie as a Christmas present the year before he died.

If a burial is to take place in a natural burial site, there are restrictions as to what can be placed in the coffin: all items must be bio-degradable and eco-friendly.

Similarly, restrictions apply should cremation be the chosen option. It is advisable to check with the funeral director as to what is permitted.

12. Do you wish your coffin to be carried in a hearse? Or is there an alternative?

> ❧
>
> *Note that although it is traditional for a hearse to be used, it is by no means compulsory. For example, an ambulance driver was carried to his grave in an ambulance; a lorry driver in his lorry, and the founder of the Body Shop, Anita Roddick, opted for a camper van.*
>
> ❧

13. Specify whether you wish your family and friends to use limousines. If so, how many and who should use them?

14. Do you have any preference as to the route which is taken to the funeral?

15. Do you wish for a notice of your passing to be placed in a newspaper's obituaries column? If so, which newspaper(s)? Or would social media be sufficient?

16. It would greatly assist your executors and family if you offered some ideas and dates for your obituary. Is there anything that you would particularly wish to have mentioned?

17. Do you have any particular likes or dislikes regarding the flowers which are used? What kind of wreath(s) would you prefer (if any)? (Consider colour/type/arrangement)?

18. Or would you prefer mourners to donate to a charity instead? If so, which charity/charities? If possible, supply the charity's registration number(s) to avoid confusion.

19. Or would you prefer donations to go towards some other form of commemoration, such as a bench or plaque? Where would you want such a commemoration to be placed?

20. Would you wish for a Requiem Mass to take place the evening before the funeral? If so, in which church?

> *Options for what happens the day prior to your funeral should be considered. Although Requiem Masses and wakes are becoming increasingly uncommon, they are by no means rare.*
>
> *Families can take great comfort from having their family member return home for one last time. It offers an unparalleled opportunity to say their goodbyes.*

21. Alternatively, would you like for your coffin to return home the night before your funeral?

22. If your funeral is to be religious, in which place of worship should it be held? If it's a Civil or Humanist Ceremony, in which venue?

23. Do you wish to have a private service for close family and friends only or can anyone attend? *(If you would prefer that certain individuals were not notified of your death, advise below.)*

> ❦
>
> *Keeping the burial or cremation as a private family affair has its advantages but bear in mind that many funeral attendees may have departed the 'send-off' before the family arrives. This can defeat the chance to meet far-flung friends, colleagues of the deceased.*
>
> *Your funeral director should be able to offer suitable solutions.*
>
> ❦

24. In terms of the attendees, do you have any preference as to the dress code? Traditional black? Colourful Hawaiian shirts? State your preference:

25. Who would you prefer to hold the Service (perhaps a particular priest, minister or celebrant)?

26. Thinking about the coffin – do you have any preference as to who the pallbearers would be? Please list. *(Note: six to eight are required.)*

27. Once inside the place where the ceremony is going to take place, is there anything you would like placed on top of the coffin?

> ℰℴℂℛ
>
> *Many places of worship will not permit flags to drape the coffin – i.e. the Union flag, Tricolour etc.*
>
> *However, many mourners place a photograph of the deceased on top of the coffin, and flowers are always popular.*
>
> *Items which were familiar to the deceased are particularly touching and evocative - such as a garden trowel, the Racing Post, a pipe, military paraphernalia, racing helmet…*
>
> *For readings, consider religious text, poetry, prose, contemporary writings or even your own words.*
>
> ℰℴℂℛ

28. Have you any preferences as to what readings, prose or poems are read at the service?

    Please list what they are and where they can be found.

    If they are unusual, you may wish to write out the text of the readings at the back of this book.

29. Your choice of music for the service or mass will create the tone and set the mood. Consider whether you wish it to be solemn and traditional, or more upbeat and celebratory. Options abound and can include everything from bagpipes or a vocalist, to tracks from CDs. This is a very personal matter, and one which others cannot easily choose. You may also need to bear in mind whether a contemporary twist on a traditional, religious funeral is acceptable to clergy members. Consider too, whether you want mourners to weep buckets of tears or, as is becoming increasingly popular, leave the service with smiles on their faces.

If you are struggling to choose, it can be a welcome gesture to ask your nearest and dearest for their thoughts. Have they any requests that would comfort them at the funeral? Think not just of your spouse or children; think too of siblings or, if they are alive, your parents; they have most likely been constants in your life too. You may also wish to think about music that could be played while people are entering and leaving the venue.

So, what are your preferences for music or hymns to be played at the service? Please list on Page 25.

Note: Many crematoria have the facility to download almost any musical piece to use in a service; churches, less so. If you are IT savvy you may wish to compile your own playlist on a CD for your funeral, wake or celebration. If you have done this, where is it?

ಠಠ

The top 10 contemporary song choices in 2023* were:

1. *Supermarket Flowers*
2. *Wind Beneath my Wings*
3. *Somewhere Over the Rainbow*
4. *Dancing in the Sky*
5. *Angels*
6. *Simply the Best*
7. *You Raise Me Up*
8. *Dancing Queen*
9. *Flying Without Wings*
10. *Angel*

The top 10 hymn choices:

1. *All Things Bright and Beautiful*
2. *Abide with Me*
3. *The Lord is my Shepherd*
4. *Amazing Grace*
5. *How Great Thou Art*
6. *Jerusalem*
7. *Morning Has Broken*
8. *Old Rugged Cross*
9. *Here I am, Lord*
10. *The Day Thou Gavest, Lord*

The top 10 classical choices:

1. *Time to Say Goodbye*
2. *Nimrod*
3. *Ave Maria*
4. *Adagio in G Minor*
5. *Canon in D*
6. *Clare de Lune*
7. *Nessun Dorma*
8. *Pie Jesu*
9. *The Lark Ascending*
10. *Gabriel's Oboe*

* Courtesy of 2023 Co-Op Funeral Music Chart.

ಠಠ

30. Do you have any preference as to who should carry out the eulogy?

31. In order to assist the eulogist, are there any pointers you would like mentioned?
    (Consider your achievements, career, hobbies, memberships of clubs/societies, important people and pivotal moments in your life, amusing stories and so on. You may wish to include dates to give some reference points to assist. Continue at the back of the book if necessary).

32. The live streaming of funerals is becoming increasingly popular offering those who live further afield the opportunity to witness the ceremony and say their own goodbyes. It can be videoed for personal use via smartphones and tablets or, with some prearranged planning, can be streamed for worldwide viewing. Most funeral directors today offer this service. Is this something you would wish to happen?

33. Having chosen the music and the readings, please list the Order of Service which you would prefer. *(Note: the following is only a suggestion. Modify your own version as you see fit).*

Entrance Music: _____

Introduction: _____

Reading 1: _____

Music: _____

Reading 2: _____

Music: _____

Eulogy: _____

The Commendation: _____

Music to leave to: _____

34. Are there any other matters you wish to raise regarding your funeral?

Let's Talk About ……Money Saving Funerals

Broaching the thorny issue of funeral costs is not for the faint-hearted. Who amongst us wishes to be seen questioning funeral fees and risk being perceived as miserly during one of life's most traumatic events? The trepidation of even mentioning the word *price* lest it offends, combined with pressure from family members for a lavish affair and a funeral director's lack of transparency on pricing and there's a recipe for overspending on a grand scale.

It's a common theme. The question I am asked more than any other is, "How can I ensure my family doesn't spend a fortune on my funeral?" The simple solution is, of course, to choose components of the funeral in advance., as you are paying for it, it is only natural that you should be able to specify how much should be spent. This, more than anything, will guide executors as to what is preferred: pennywise prudence or a splendid splash.

While it is important to recognise that we get just one send-off; (it is, after all, literally a once in a lifetime event), the average person will arrange just two funerals in their lifetime and few will be sufficiently practised to make savvy decisions. While there's nothing wrong with having a grand send off, it should ideally be done with some forethought and consideration.

As with most large purchases in life, it's the added extras, the incidentals that drive up costs, so what can we do to reduce the outlay without compromising on quality and style? Here are a few ideas to help you make informed choices. If any of the points appeal, you may wish to circle the number, to guide your executors or funeral planners.

1. According to the Dying Matters Coalition, fewer than ten per cent of us bother to shop around for quotes. The time to do this isn't after a death, it's now. So, if you are interested in saving money, make a list of your requirements and call two or three local funeral directors so you can compare like with like. Fees can vary enormously, often with thousands of pounds differential. Generally speaking, small independent funeral directors are the most competitive.

2. At the time of going to press, the average cost of a basic funeral followed by burial in the UK is £4,794*. Burial is always going to be more expensive than cremation as a burial plot has to be purchased and, in addition, there are grave diggers fees.

3. The average cost of a funeral followed by cremation is £3,673*. Keep in mind, fees are dependent on not just the day of the week but also the time of day that the service in the crematorium is held.
To put it into context, the City of London crematorium fees for 2022-2023 ranged from £560 to £1,492 depending on the time of day. It cost £560 for a 30-minute service between 8.30 – 10.00 am but £1,040 for the same service after 10.00 am.

4. Coffins: the range is vast; from eco-cardboard at £100 to oak caskets at £2,000. They can be purchased directly from wholesalers if you wish to go down the DIY route, although some funeral directors will not use supplied coffins and you need to consider delivery costs too. Also, if you are going to opt for a green funeral, note that there are many grades of cardboard so don't stint on something which is, frankly, unserviceable. The unthinkable has been known to happen.

5. If a body is not going to be viewed, there is little to be gained in paying for embalming. And, if the deceased wished to be buried in a natural burial ground or at sea, it is prohibited anyway. Many Funeral Directors carry out embalming as a matter of course, unless you stipulate otherwise. It is unnecessary. Save around £150.

6. Dressing: Most of us have wardrobes full of clothes. There should be no need to purchase a funeral gown or suit. It costs around £150 to dress the body.

7. Is the deceased going to be visited at the Funeral Director's premises? If not, ensure you are not paying for something that is not required.

8. For some, the deceased resting in church overnight prior to a funeral is a given. Perfectly acceptable, but bear in mind there are extra charges involved for the hiring of the church. There will also be an additional day's hire of a hearse. Similar fees will apply should you wish to bring the deceased home.

9. There are few better examples of waste than the money collectively spent on funeral flowers which are hugely expensive. Arrange instead for the family to contribute to a single wreath. Go large if need be and purchase a fabulous one to cover the entire coffin. It will cost £250-£300 but it will be much cheaper than everyone buying individual wreaths.

10. Or…sometimes less is more. One of the most stunning floral tributes I have witnessed was a rattan coffin with lilies loosely stitched around the edges and rose petals strewn on top of the coffin. Beautifully simple and simply beautiful. Nip to the local florist and it will cost around £30.

NOTE: Specify 'No Flowers' to mourners and they can contribute instead to a charity of the deceased's choice. A fantastic opportunity to raise funds, but be ready! If donations aren't collected on the way out of the funeral service, chances are they never will be.

11. A hearse and pallbearers will cost around £500-£600 for the day's hire. Alternatives are available: any estate car or, to keep in line with the independently minded, consider a self-drive hearse. Not only will this be cheaper, it also offers the family the opportunity to take control and specify, no matter how wayward, the route of the coffin. Does the family really need a limousine at around £225 each? Apparently, fewer of us are using them and following the hearse in our own cars.

12. Do you need a celebrant? If you are not religious, you may have willing family members or friends who are capable of offering a poignant, intimate and fitting tribute. Be careful, it can be emotionally daunting. Letting a sensitive, skilled professional celebrant manage proceedings can pay dividends resulting in a well-planned, memorable day. Celebrant fees: £200-£250.

13. Orders of Service: Anyone can purchase 300 gsm card and, with the necessary computer skills, print it. Alternatively, order online for around £0.75 each as opposed to the Funerals Director's £2.00 - £2.50 each. There are templates online for Orders of Service.

14. Funeral music. Obviously, the hire of an organist, choir or soloist is not without cost, but canned music is not always the answer either. If the choice of music is secular or classical, enquire first whether the clergy will allow it. Check too the quality of the acoustics – particularly if the funeral is being held in a church or small venue: not all have *BOSE* sound systems, so it may prove to be a false economy. Remember, this isn't about sacrificing quality; you have just one opportunity to get it right.

15. The send-off: it's entirely optional and options abound: DIY at home or use a hotel, pub or church hall. Prices will, of course, vary enormously but, for many, this is one of the most important elements of the funeral. Memories of the deceased shared, friendships rekindled, links forged, heartfelt anecdotes from those unwilling or unable to speak at the funeral, revealed. In 2022, the average spend was £467* (includes both catering and venue hire).
Pubs and hotels charge around £10 - £15 per head, but if you have a suitable venue, platters of sandwiches cost just £20 - £25**.
Many are choosing to forget the free bar.

16. For those with no religious beliefs who would prefer to have no funeral at all, choose a simple Direct Cremation. In 2022, 18%* of cremations were not preceded by any service at all – a trend which is becoming increasingly popular. The average cost is £1,511* but shop around and you will find lower still: £795** plus disbursements. (www.col.co.uk) See Page 33.

17. Donate your body to medical science. There's no funeral required and the medical schools will pay for a short service and cremation but be aware that not all bodies are accepted and it may take up to three years before a service is held. See Page 45.

18. In 2022, families spent an average of £157* on individual memorial, death and funeral notices in newspapers. All add to the overall cost. Attempt if you can, to consolidate notices. Alternatively, with fewer newspaper readers today, consider getting the word out through social media.

19. For those who are in receipt of Government benefits or tax credits, there may be the opportunity to apply for assistance in the shape of a one-off Funeral Expenses Payment which can be up to £1,000** but be aware that payment can be slow in arriving. (www.gov.uk/funeral-payments).

20. There is also the possibility of Bereavement Support Payments for those under state pension age. The maximum payment is up to £2,500** plus up to 18 £100 monthly payments (but more for Child Benefit eligibility) and the deceased needs to have paid sufficient National Insurance contributions to qualify. To receive all the benefits the spouse/civil partner must claim within three months of a partner's death.   (www.gov.uk/bereavement-payment/eligibility)

Funerals should always be a fitting and meaningful tribute, but the amount of money spent should not be seen as an indicator of how cherished the deceased was. Unquestionably, the cost of a funeral should never be the overriding factor but, as we all know, paying suitable respect to the deceased does not mean that every last vestige of common sense should be cast adrift. With prudence, strategic choices and some careful forward planning, unnecessary costs can be avoided making life, and death, more financially manageable for all.

* Source: The SunLife Cost of Dying Report 2023   ** 2023 prices

Additional Notes

FUNERALS

> Ensure your Executors know where to find your Will and Last Orders containing your funeral wishes.
>
> I thank the gentleman who advised me that his were stored on top of his wardrobe.
> Hmmm....

SECTION FOUR

Grave Thoughts

In 2022, around 25 per cent of deaths in the UK were followed by a burial. For many of the bereaved, having the opportunity to visit and tend a grave can offer a crumb of comfort, particularly in the first years after loss. For those planning their own funeral, if one's spouse has already been buried, there's a natural resting place already waiting.

One would imagine that choosing the location of a burial plot is straightforward enough; recent media headlines suggest otherwise. Today's complex family ties and divided loyalties are bringing with them their own set of unique disputes. Siblings in disagreement over rival religions' cemeteries for a parent, family members at odds as to whether to bury or cremate a parent and twice and thrice-married spouses with torn loyalties as to where - and with whom - they would like to be buried, have all made the news. And disputes can wrangle on for years. All of which, one imagines, would cause the deceased nothing but despair were they to see the fallout. Clearly, this would be the last thing anyone would wish for, so everything that can be decided upon ahead of time is in everyone's interest. If you think that your choice of location for your burial could, for whatever reason, prove to be contentious, discuss it with your family now whilst you have the ability to calm potentially troubled waters.

As space in cemeteries dwindles, burial plots are becoming increasingly costly and range considerably in price. The national average is around for burial plot £750 for a burial plot plus other burial fees of £600. According to the website Beyond, the most expensive location for a burial plot was in Highgate Cemetery in London at £19,975. Why wouldn't it be when you could potentially have George Michael, Karl Marx and George Eliot as neighbours? The cheapest funeral and burial was in Belfast at £3,317.

Burial plots are leased for 25, 50, 75 or 100 years depending on the local authority but, as plots become increasingly scarce, some authorities are starting to exercise their rights to reclaim plots so that they can re-use and re-inter. You may wish to check the costs and the duration of the leases in nearby cemeteries before deciding where to be buried. Having selected the cemetery, you may also wish to choose the location of the plot. Those next to the pathways or near a bench are usually slightly more expensive.

Natural, Woodland and Green Burial

Natural, woodland or green burial grounds are becoming increasingly popular and are seen as an environmentally friendly alternative for those who aren't religious; they create a tranquil area of peace where local wildlife can flourish. The grounds are supposed to look natural and that, by definition, precludes the tending of a grave. If your loved ones are enthusiastic gardeners and would be keen to deck the grave with flowers, shrubs, bulbs, balloons and suchlike, you may need to reconsider.

There are usually a few restrictions as to the demarcation of the grave too: some allow a wooden plaque, some require that plaques are placed flat at ground level so that they don't protrude and detract from the landscape, others do not allow markers at all. There are further issues to take into account: embalming is prohibited, the coffin will need to be eco-friendly and there are restrictions as to what can be included within the coffin itself. These types of burial grounds are still relatively sparse nationwide, so you may need to research the location of such sites.

> ### DID YOU KNOW
>
> *…you can be buried at sea? At the time of going to press, it costs around £6,000. There are significant regulations to adhere to: you will need a special sea coffin, no embalmment is allowed, a GP's certificate must state that the remains are free from fever and infection, a biodegradable shroud must be used, and a license from the Marine Maritime Organisation is required. Go to www.gov.uk and type 'burial at sea' into the search box.*
>
> *Sir Francis Drake was buried at sea in full armour. Osama Bin Laden also has a watery grave – perhaps for entirely different reasons.*

1. Where would you like to be buried?
   State too the cemetery's religion if applicable.

2. Have you purchased a plot, or is there an existing plot available for you? What is the plot number? Where is the documentation to verify this?

3. It is becoming increasingly popular for music to be played, or balloons to be released at the end of the graveside service. At the final interment, do you wish for anything special to happen?

4. Do you have any preference as to which type of headstone is used to mark the grave?

5. Is there anything in particular you would like to have inscribed on the headstone? Is there anything you would prefer to omit?

The choice of epitaph on a headstone can be thought-provoking and even pithy. Frank Sinatra's has "The Best is yet to Come" on his headstone.

Irish-born and former Goon, Spike Milligan, requested the inscription, "I told you I was ill" on his headstone. However, the Diocese of Chichester, where his grave is, had issues with the request. His family agreed to inscribe the epitaph in Gaelic instead. Stephen Hawking, the physicist, asked for his equation:

$$S = \frac{\pi A k c^3}{2hG}$$

for black holes to be placed on his tombstone which which is in Westminster Abbey in London.

SECTION FIVE

ಸಿಂ

Cremation

In the United Kingdom, around 75 per cent of deaths are followed by a cremation. There would appear to be sound reasons too: it's considered to be environmentally friendly and, with a national shortage of burial plots, it is socially responsible too. It happens to be the least expensive option too.

Cremation Fees

The 2018 Competitions and Market Authority's report on the Funerals Sector found that cremation fees had risen by 84 per cent in the previous ten years; a trend that continues year on year. Prices are wide-ranging and the variation is not just postcode-related but also dependent on whether the local crematorium is one of the UK's 101 privately-owned. These are not only increasing in number but, having a local monopoly, are choosing to drive costs up, arguably in order to sell their sister company's funeral plans. Less expensive is the 185 local authority-owned non-profit-making crematoria which are seen as offering a service to the community.

There are other pricing factors involved: the time and day that the service takes place, its length and, in the case of local authority crematoria, whether the deceased lived within the borough. Most crematoria have options of 30, 45 and 60 minutes services, so should you wish to avoid the appearance of a tube-train station at rush hour, opt for a 60 minutes service which should offer everyone a little more time for reflection.

> *Top of the cost charts in the 2021 Cremation Fee League Table was Friockheim in Scotland at £1,100* with Chichester a close second at £1,077. The cheapest was Belfast at £392. **
> **The 2021 Cremation Society of Great Britain Report.*

Direct Cremation

For non-believers or those who do not want a funeral service of any kind, consider direct cremation which is, essentially, a no-frills option for those who prefer simplicity. Initially it was introduced with a view to keeping costs down to assist the financially challenged but, there is anecdotal evidence to suggest that they are becoming increasingly popular due to TV advertisement campaigns. In 2022, around 20 per cent of all cremations were direct cremations.

It's a relatively smooth operation: the funeral director collects the remains of the deceased in a simple coffin and the cremation takes place without a ceremony, hearse, limousines or flowers. The ashes are delivered back to the family within a relatively short space of time. Thereafter, the family can choose when - or indeed whether - to hold a service of remembrance or celebratory gathering, at a time and location of their choosing, in the presence of the ashes, with the deceased's loved ones present.

Often, the financial saving isn't the overriding factor for choosing this option; it is that this form of cremation can provide far-flung families with a flexibility which other funerals cannot. It also offers a simplified, understated affair for those who have no religious beliefs. I have had more people tell me than I ever thought possible that this would be their preferred choice. They are in good company: both David Bowie and John Lennon had direct cremations.

Disposing of Ashes

Options abound as to how to dispose of ashes. They can be buried within a woodland site, a crematorium or, whether you have an existing plot or not, a cemetery. You can bury them in the back garden in a pot or urn so that loved ones can take them with them should they move home. They can be made into jewellery, cufflinks and crystal paperweights. They can be scattered within remembrance gardens or a favourite location although you should seek permission from the landowner before scattering on private property.

For those who have a yearning for water, (as did Janis Joplin, Robin Williams, Neil Armstrong and Alfred Hitchcock), there's no special permission required for the scattering of ashes at sea although it's wise to stand upwind before scattering or use a practical biodegradable ash urn.

Star Trek creator Gene Roddenberry and actor James Doohan, who played Scottie in the same cult TV series, both had their ashes sent into outer space.

If that is a bridge too far, ashes can be put into fireworks to guarantee spectacular and memorable event.

If you have chosen to be cremated, and before you inflict your desire to have your ashes fashioned into custom-made jewellery for each of your offspring, it would be useful to hold a discussion and together decide what you would like to happen.

1. Do you have any preference as to which crematorium is used?

2. What do you wish to happen to your ashes? If you wish your ashes to be scattered or buried, say where:

3. You may choose to erect a plaque at a cemetery or a crematorium.
   What inscription do you wish to have? Also, consider whether there is anything you wish to omit.

SECTION SIX

After Thoughts...

1. Have you considered whether you would like for the mourners to meet after the funeral? If so, where?

2. Do you have any preferences as to what is (or isn't) served after the funeral? If so, please specify: Consider too whether you would like to offer a free bar, tea and coffee or anything at all.

SECTION SEVEN

Medical Matters

We all know that life can bring simple joys and minor miracles at the most unexpected moments. Equally, we are at the mercy of unforeseen events which can prove bewildering. Few of us remain unscathed without the sudden loss of a loved one. Fewer still feel prepared to put our own house in order.

Choosing to complete a book such as this, will take a considerable amount of thought and energy. No one wishes to think of a time when these notes will be brought to light and needed by our executors and family. Take heart, any discomfort you feel should be alleviated by the fact that you are undoubtedly going some considerable way to assist the people you care about most, at a time when they will need your help most. Completing this book for worst case scenarios is one thing, but there is also the need to consider and make provision for the possibility of a long-term illness which could compromise your abilities.

Illness and disability come in all manner of guises. The diagnosis of a life-threatening condition may well focus the mind for some but for others, the capacity to think straight is impaired by the shock and distress that such news can bring. Combine that with the side effects that various forms of treatment and medication can produce, and rather than being incentivised into getting one's affairs in order, any motivation you once fostered, may be completely eroded.

While life expectancy in the UK has increased, healthy life expectancy has not. Our longevity is often compromised by poor health and medical complications. Some illnesses, such as dementia, are incremental and barely discernible until the condition has advanced so greatly that the ability to focus the mind has diminished, and all thoughts of Wills and Letters of Wishes are far removed from one's concerns. Whilst that may be an irrelevance for the sufferer, neglecting to tackle the issue ahead of time can leave significant difficulties for the family who would be the ones having to cope with complex health and financial issues. Unquestionably then, the best time to get affairs in order is when one has the time, wherewithal and mental capacity required to think clearly.

Whilst long-term illness is one thing, none of us can rule out the possibility of a life-changing accident which impairs one's physical or mental capacity forever or worse still, proves fatal. The randomness of life means that such an event could happen to anyone, regardless of age. In an ideal world, every responsible adult should consider getting at least some of their affairs in order by stating their wishes.

There are a number of practical steps which can be taken to safeguard you, your family and your potential future carers. A suitably qualified solicitor or professional Will-writer should be able to advise and deal with these matters sensitively but here are some things you may wish to consider.

Advance Decisions / Living Wills

An Advance Decision (also known as a Living Will) can be used to record the type of care that you are prepared to refuse were you, for example, to become unable, through illness, to make or communicate decisions for yourself. It advises your doctors, carers and family members about the various, but very specific, medical treatment which you would wish to refuse to sustain life. Each individual type of treatment must be named so that there is no doubt as to which particular care it is that you wish to refuse. It is important that you discuss this with family members, so they are aware of your wishes. Without that conversation, they are likely to have strong objections to the refusal or denial of treatment should the situation arise.

If the Advance Decision is made at a time when the individual has the mental capacity to make it, it is legally binding. It can be spoken or written but be aware that while verbal instructions are valid, they are more likely to be overlooked. Doctors have a legal, medical obligation to treat you, so if any part of your Advance Decision is ambiguous or incomplete, medical staff have the right to ignore the instructions laid out.

Advance Decisions can be completed by a solicitor specialising in end-of-life issues. Alternatively, as long as it is clearly stated and relevant to the medical circumstances that may arise, you can write a less formal statement yourself. To avoid any confusion or misunderstandings, it would be advisable to discuss the matter fully with your GP, your medical team and solicitor and ask them to inspect the document. Once done, you must sign each copy of your Advance Decision, date it and ensure it is signed by an independent witness.

Copies should be kept:

- alongside your Will
- with your GP
- with hospital medical staff (where applicable)
- with family, a friend or one of the executors of your Will
- and, if you have one, your health and welfare attorney under a Lasting Power of Attorney.

As with a Will, an Advance Decision should be reviewed periodically and, if you wish, revised as circumstances or attitudes change and, potentially, medical advancements are made. Revisions made will need to be freshly signed, dated and once again, signed by an independent witness. All changes should also be noted with your doctor and your family, along with the other holders of your statement listed above.

1. Have you made an Advance Decision/ Living Will? If so, where is the paperwork?

2. Who has a copy of it?

3. Have you discussed your Advance Decision/Living Will with your family? Whom have you told?

Advance Statement

Whilst an Advance Decision offers the opportunity to refuse medical treatment, an Advance Statement allows you to choose the care you would wish to receive should the time come when you cannot communicate your thoughts. In it, you can convey your personal preferences and wishes in terms of your values, beliefs, religion and the preferred location for your care. You can advise about the more practical issues too, such as whether you have allergies, your dietary requirements, the type of things that please you or make you uneasy – any or all of which would make you more comfortable. You may even wish to state whether you would wish to be visited by friends and family in the last days or weeks of your life, particularly if you were to be severely incapacitated. You may, for example, prefer privacy.

An Advance Statement is not legally binding but, by providing this information, you will be assisting those who are charged with caring for you, who may need to make decisions on your behalf.

You can draft your own Advance Statement. Once signed, ensure that your GP, carer, family and medical staff treating you have a copy, so that they are aware of your wishes and concerns.

4.   Have you made an Advance Statement? If so, where is it, and who knows about it?

Lasting Powers of Attorney

A Lasting Power of Attorney (LPA) is a legal document which allows you to appoint one or more trusted individuals (attorneys) to take care of you, your health and/or your finances should you, at some time in the future, lack the mental capacity to make such decisions. While you are able, you can put guidelines in place for them now. The LPA replaced the Enduring Power of Attorney (EPA) in 2007, but EPAs made before that date are still valid.

If you do not have LPAs in place, medical professionals and social workers, who do not know you, can make decisions on your behalf, while the Court of Protection appoints a Deputy to manage your affairs under the court's supervision. This can be time-consuming, intensely frustrating and stressful for your family. The process can be extremely expensive too – particularly if a solicitor is acting for you - and can be more expensive than putting the LPAs in place at the outset.

There are two types of LPA:

- Health and Welfare
- Property and Financial Affairs

Health and Welfare LPA

A Health and Welfare Lasting Power of Attorney allows you to appoint one or more attorneys who can make decisions on your behalf about the kind of care, support and medical treatment you receive; it also includes consenting to or refusing life-sustaining treatment. Your attorneys can also oversee where you live and your day-to-day routine, which could and should greatly enhance the quality of your life. They can only make such decisions on your behalf if, in the future, you lack the ability to make decisions for yourself.

It can take up to twenty weeks for an LPA to be registered with the Office of the Public Guardian providing there are no mistakes made in the application.

5. Have you a Health and Welfare LPA in place? When was it made? Who is/are the attorney(s) and where is the paperwork?

DID YOU KNOW?

While many people use professionals such as solicitors or Will writers to apply for LPAs, you can apply online via the government website: www.gov.uk Type LPA into the Search box. The forms aren't complicated.

At the time of going to press, the cost of registering each LPA is £82. This can be reduced or exempted should you have a low income and/or be registered for state benefits. Complete form LPA 120A.

6. Have you written any instructions to assist your attorney? Where are they?

> **DID YOU KNOW?**
>
> *If you already have LPAs and they were registered between April 2013 and March 2017, the Office of the Public Guardian is refunding between £34 and £54 per document.*
>
> *If you think that this applies to you, you can start your claim by phoning 0300 456 0300.*

Property and Financial Affairs LPA

A Property and Financial LPA allows you to appoint one or more attorneys and grants them the legal authority to make some or all of the decisions about your finances. They can determine what happens in the buying, selling and maintenance of your property, your financial affairs, operating your bank accounts, investments, dealing with the Inland Revenue, sorting out state benefits and so on.

The LPA, once registered, does not have to come into force immediately; it can, should you choose, only take effect if or when you lose the capacity to deal with any or all of these issues yourself.

7. Do you have a Property and Financial Affairs LPA? If so, who is/are the appointed attorney(s) and where is the paperwork?

8. Have you written any instructions to assist your attorney(s) in respect of the Property and Financial Affairs LPA? Where are they?

Let's Talk About…… Organ Donation

Some years ago, I saw a compelling item on the TV on an issue which, at the time, was completely off my radar. It told the story of a young lad of just ten years of age who had died in a car crash four years earlier. He was a beautiful blond-haired child who would have grown up to be a very handsome man. It was difficult not to be moved, seeing the loss of the potential… until I heard the rest of the story. His dying wish was that his organs were used to assist others. The result was that nine people benefitted from his generosity.

To celebrate his birthday annually, his parents held a party in remembrance of their dead son and they invite the same nine people who have received his organs to attend. Each of the recipients' lives had been either transformed, enriched or eased and their gratitude was, and is, immense. For the parents, the closest they get to being in their dead child's presence - however remotely - is group-hugging the recipients.

One cannot help but be touched by the generosity of the young lad wishing to help those he had never met, but one shouldn't overlook the pivotal role his parents played. They adhered to their son's wishes at a time when they were racked with grief. Today, that despair is marginally alleviated by listening to their son's heart still beating, his lungs still breathing and liver thriving, living, assisting and offering life to those recipients. His parents had, in effect, given away something that they had cherished but which would have gone, quite literally, to ground. The recipients' lives have been transformed. A win-win.

★ ★ ★

Every year, hundreds of people die due to a shortage of replacement organs but thanks to successful campaigns, organ donation has started to penetrate the national consciousness. In 2020, new legislation, Max and Keira's Law, a donation scheme which became law in England, has altered the way in which organ donation takes place. It was brought about when a young boy, Max Johnson, received the donated heart of a nine-year-old girl, Keira Ball, after she was involved in a fatal road accident. These two children have together, in their young lives changed so many more. Organ donation consent is now presumed on death unless the person has opted out of the donation scheme or the deceased's family overrules the donation. Scotland, Wales and Northern Ireland all have similar schemes in place.

Whilst this new law is undeniably a step in the right direction, there is still room for improvement. According to the Organ Donation Register (ODR), only 41 per cent of us have proactively registered as potential donors and, given that your donation would be reliant on your loved ones' consent at the crucial time, there is still the need to verify your wishes with your nearest and dearest, in your Letter of Wishes or a conversation.

Few of us manage to do that, so, we still appear to be falling short. The unwillingness, or even the inability, to discuss end-of-life issues with family members means that when the time comes, many families are unaware of the deceased's wishes and they either unwittingly or consciously disregard them. Even with the new legislation, families still have the option, at that most crucial of moments, to quash the donation, regardless of the default position of the new law or the deceased's wishes.

So why do families, who have the ultimate say, refuse to give not just *their* permission, but ignore the wishes of the deceased? Most likely, it is because the last thing any family wants at a time of deep sorrow, is to be pressurised into making rash, complex decisions. Without a conversation explaining and verifying ones wishes, leaving loved ones to make such a key decision while in a state of shock and profound heartache is a step too far. Unfortunately, within days, those who have ignored the deceased's wishes often regret their decision. But by then it is too late. They can carry the burden of knowing they did not honour the deceased's wishes for decades.

We know that adhering to a loved one's wishes can assist in both the healing and the grieving process so perhaps it is time for us to create our own win-win situation. By opening up the conversation about your own donation wishes now, you will undoubtedly assist your family in the future. Otherwise, how would they deal with the issue at a moment's notice? Would they know?

Organ Donation

1. Have you opted-in or opted-out as an Organ Donor? Have you got a card to verify this and if so, where is it?

> **DID YOU KNOW?**
>
> One organ donor can save or transform up to nine lives. There are currently around 6,500 people in the UK on the active waiting list.
>
> There is no age limit on organ donation.
> The oldest recorded solid organ UK donor was 83.
> The oldest recorded UK recipient was 85.
> The oldest recorded UK cornea donor was 107.

2. Have you discussed organ donation with your family? When did this conversation take place?

3. Which family members have you informed?

Leaving Your Body to Medical Science

> ❧
>
> IMPORTANT!!
>
> *If you wish to donate your organs or leave your body to medical science, it is crucial that you advise your family, GP, solicitor and your executors so they can make informed decisions when the time comes.*
>
> *If you are leaving your body to medical science, they will need to ensure the body is embalmed within five days of death.*
>
> ☙

You may wish to consider donating your body to medical science. The Human Tissue Authority has an ongoing need for human bodies to assist in the education and training of, amongst others, doctors, surgeons, dentists, forensic specialists and neuroscientists. For many donors, it is a selfless and generous act used as a means to give something back to society; a willingness to contribute to medical research which will, in turn, assist future generations.

Bequeathing one's body is not the same as donating organs. It is therefore important that you state your preference between organ and body donation. Cadavers must remain intact; so, if organs have been used for transplantation or if a post-mortem has been performed, it will rule out the possibility of body donation. Once all parts of the body have been used, some schools may pay for a simple funeral and cremation for the donor, some will offer the option for the family to take possession of the ashes, others offer a single service for groups of those who have bequeathed their body.

Before choosing to donate your body, discuss the matter with your family as they will need to be aware of the implications. It can take up to three years before all parts of the body are used and that, in itself, can delay the grieving process and prevent closure.

If donating your body interests you, contact your nearest regional medical school. (Details at the back of the book). Each school has different procedures and acceptance policies, so you can familiarise yourself with the criteria before completing the necessary forms. Have you registered to donate your body to The Human Tissue Authority? Where is the paperwork?

Additional Notes

SECTION EIGHT

Where There's A Will

1. Have you made a Will? If so, when was it made?

2. Have you made any amendments (codicils) to your Will? If so, when was the last one made?

3. Where is your Will? If it is held at your solicitor's or Will writer's office? If so, please supply their contact details:

Name:

Address:

Telephone nos:

Email address:

> ### EXECUTORS
>
> *If you cannot locate a Will, consider checking with the solicitor or Will-writer who drafted it, the London Probate Department (Register of Wills) or Certainty. Addresses are at the back of this book.*

4. If it is not there, where is it?

Your executors **must** know where to locate it.

(NB. Do not leave your Will in a bank safety deposit box. It will be inaccessible without Grant of Probate which cannot be obtained without access to the Will.)

> **DID YOU KNOW?**
>
> In England and Wales, executors can now apply for probate online through a government scheme launched in 2019. Go to www.gov.uk and type 'Apply for Probate Online' into the search box.

5. For the sake of completeness, who are your executors? Supply names, addresses, telephone numbers (home, work and mobile) and email addresses of each:

Executor 1's Name: _____

Address: _____

Telephone nos: _____

Email address: _____

Executor 2's Name: _____

Address: _____

Telephone nos: _____

Email address: _____

Executor 3's Name:

Address:

Telephone nos:

Email address:

Executor 4's Name:

Address:

Telephone nos:

Email address:

6. Is each executor aware of the location and the content of your Will? (There is no need to inform them or any of your beneficiaries about your Will's contents, if you do not wish to.)

7. Are your executors aware that you have completed this book?
If not, advise them and mention its location. Consider the Immediate Tick List on page 1.

8. Have you written on your computer or the internet, any other Letters of Wishes? If so, where are they? Can your executors access them?

9. Have you set up a trust fund which will come into force under your Will?

10. Who set it up? Supply the name and address of the professional.

11. Who are the trustees? Supply their contact details:

12. Have you given instructions as to how the trust should be administered after death? Where are these instructions?

SECTION NINE

Money Matters

One of the most important tasks your executors will have to carry out is to apply for a Grant of Probate, the Probate Registry document which authorises executors to administer the estate. In the first instance, and in order to apply, your executors will have to identify and declare the value of your estate; that is, the sum of your assets and possessions minus your outstanding debts.

Wills generally do not chart the individual assets of the Will-maker and, given that the onus is on your executors to ensure all your assets are accounted for prior to the application, they will need your assistance. There should be no greater incentive for you to get your accounts in order, than the thought of your hard-earned money languishing, unclaimed, because it remains undiscovered.

Assets

Your executors will initially need to provide proof of your estate's gross value; that is, the sum of your finances, possessions and, if you own your own home, its market value. They will need to ascertain the value of any endowment, assurance and life insurance policies you have, as well as lump sums from annuities and pensions that are payable on death.

EXECUTORS

You will need to provide proof of the value of the deceased's property which can easily be obtained from an estate agent.

In an effort to gain maximum Inheritance Tax, (IHT) it is not unheard of for HMRC to challenge the valuation if it believes the property has been undervalued.

Conversely, if the property has been overvalued and does not achieve the declared amount when sold, there is the potential to claim back overpaid IHT. Use form IHT38.

> *In the UK, reports estimate that between £15 and £77 billion of assets lay unclaimed because executors and families cannot locate them. Given the proliferation of online accounts and our changing lifestyle, this is likely to be the tip of the iceberg.*
>
> *If you think you have misplaced or simply forgotten about the existence of a bank, building society or National Savings account, contact www.mylostaccount.co.uk or the Unclaimed Assets Register www.uar.co.uk to find lost funds before completing this book.*
>
> *Similarly, if you have lost or mislaid pension paperwork, you can contact the free Pension Tracing Service at www.gov.uk Type Lost Pension into the search box or telephone 0800 731 0193.*
>
> *Executors can also check prior to applying for probate. The information on Page 3 may be useful.*

Stocks and shares, premium bonds, foreign assets and any high-value items (such as jewllery, cars, artwork etc) will also need to be included.

It sounds simple enough, but whilst paperwork within a property may be relatively easy to locate, making sense of the innumerable statements, bills and invoices, any or all of which may be outdated, is not easy. Paperwork will need to be sieved through methodically as even old statements could highlight a forgotten asset. It can be an extremely time-consuming task for executors, particularly if paperwork isn't in order or they are not acquainted with your finances. If you live alone and no one is familiar with your assets, multiply that challenge tenfold.

Finding bank statements, policy and pension paperwork is one thing; but what if there is no paperwork to uncover? The continual pressure from financial institutions for customers to go 'paperless' certainly helps to save the rainforests but, for the consumer, it increases the likelihood of accounts and policies going undiscovered.

Take some time now to assist your executors to uncover your assets. On the following pages, catalogue the policies, accounts and all the pension plans (both private and workplace) which you have invested in throughout your life. For security reasons, do not list bank account numbers here; it will be sufficient to list the sorting code. List too where they will find the original paperwork.

➢ Before you start, photocopy the forms on the following pages prior to completion so you can update them in the future.
➢ Complete the details of your bank account(s) and assets on page 53.
➢ Place any welcome introductory letter from a bank or policy into your document box to highlight its existence.
➢ Complete too the Insurance/Assurance/Policy form on Page 54.
➢ Find valuation certificates or receipts for high-value items you own and place in your document box.

This section is particularly important and it is strongly recommended that you regularly review it.

ASSETS FORM	BANK SORT CODE CONTACT DETAILS	LOCATION OF PAPERERWORK	
Bank Account (1) Only mention branch			
Bank Account (2) Only mention branch			
Bank Account (3) Only mention branch			
Bank Account (4) Only mention branch			
Postal Account			
Building Society (1) Only mention branch			
Building Society (2) Only mention branch			
PEPs/ TESSAs			
ISA/Bonds etc.			
Premium Bonds			
Pension Provider (1)			
Pension Provider (2)			
Annuity Provider			
Foreign/Offshore Bank Account			
Foreign Assets/Shares			

/   /   DATE

MONEY MATTERS

MONEY MATTERS

INSURANCE POLICIES FORM	INSURER/ POLICY NO.	LOCATION OF PAPERWORK
Home Insurance		
Contents Insurance		
Life Insurance		
Life Assurance		
Endowment Policy		
Health Insurance		
Dental Insurance		
Annual Travel Insurance		
Car Insurance		

/ / DATE

DIGITAL ASSETS

The term digital assets, put simply, refers to digital files which are stored online and accessed through the internet. These include accounts, cloud storage, blogs and almost any online account that requires you to log in to access them. Ensuring your executors are aware of these accounts is key if they are to uncover your personal – and potentially – professional records.

Online Accounts

For those of us who have embraced technology, the internet is our financial oyster and, driven by experts' advice on attractive interest rates, we each potentially have multiple online bank and building society accounts. If those accounts are paperless and aren't bookmarked on your computer(s) tablets or mobile phone, your executors will almost certainly have a challenge uncovering their existence.

Don't forget too, the less obvious online monetary accounts such as PayPal, bitcoin and – should you like a flutter online – gambling accounts. All will need to be uncovered, assessed and included in the estate.

Other Digital Assets

Other non-monetary digital assets include documents, images and videos that are stored online. As outlined in the Contacts section, these are often personal items, stored on social media, which have little or no financial value but can become priceless for a family after a death. The user licences for these platforms invariably expire on death but to ensure those personal items are not lost forever, you can download them onto your computer now for your family and executors to access at a later date.

You may have a library of eBooks, a compilation of musical works and a catalogue of films all of which you have 'purchased' and

---

TO DO LIST

Consider tidying up your assets: consolidate funds by closing dormant bank and building society accounts.

Unless there are disputes to settle, discard tax paperwork over 6 years old and utility bills over 2 years old.

While spring cleaning, you may wish to tidy up your computer: delete old social media contacts and forum chat rooms that are no longer relevant and remove bookmarks which are no longer required.

If you have a spouse, a civil partner or a cohabitee with whom you share utility bills, telephone, TV, car, insurance premiums, council tax, etc, one of the simplest things you can do now is to ensure that these accounts are in joint names.

The death of a partner brings many challenges. Those woes do not need to be amplified by having them wrestle with service providers because they aren't the account holder. It is an unnecessary stress.

downloaded. Kindle eBooks, iBooks and iTunes all remain the property of the 'sellers'. In legal terms, you have merely purchased the license to enjoy them during your lifetime. They, and their associated accounts, are not transferrable to anyone. However, see Mr Rycroft's useful suggestion below.

For those who use 'clouds' to store documents, insurance policy paperwork, videos and more, your executors will need to retrieve useful and potentially crucial information. How easy is it for your executors to gain access? How will they even know to look?

- Complete the form on page 57 on online accounts. If applicable, note which device serves which activity.

Income Streams

Online activity can, for some, provide an income stream and the value of that activity should be considered as part of the estate. If you have an online business of any kind, a website domain name, work for which you hold the copyright (images, photographs, articles, videos on YouTube and suchlike) or if you are a blogger and/or vlogger, your executors will need to ascertain the value and resale value of your work.

- Ensure that you read and complete the Business Section on Page 62

If you download films, music or e-books onto an external hard-drive, MP3 Player or Kindle, you could then pass on this tangible asset. You're not however, allowed to pass on these assets digitally – say via email.

Gary Rycroft, Partner
Private Client Department at
Joseph A Jones & Co LLP, Lancaster.

ONLINE/DIGITAL ASSETS FORM	LOCATION OF PAPREWORK, POLICY NO	OTHER INFORMATION. WHICH DEVICE USED?
Online Bank Account (1)		
Online Bank Account (2)		
Paypal Account		
Betting Account		
Store Loyalty Card(s)		
Air Miles Account(s)		

/ / DATE

MONEY MATTERS

Loyalty Points

Many of us are members of retail store and online loyalty schemes, some of which reward us for our custom. If this applies to you, it is important that your executors know of their existence. Some store schemes, such as Boots Advantage, Tesco Clubcard and Nectar will allow points to be transferred to a family member after a death, Marks and Spencer's Sparks will not. Avios, the Airmiles people, assess each case individually. For travellers, there may be any number of individual frequent flyer accounts and schemes for your executors to uncover.

➢ Complete the form on Page 57.

Liabilities and Loans

As well as providing details of your assets, your executors will have to establish whether you have any loans, overdrafts, mortgage(s), payment or tax arrears, bills, credit card arrears and debts. It is important that your executors are aware of these liabilities to ensure that your estate is solvent prior to the distribution of the estate. If your liabilities outweigh your assets, they should seek professional advice.

➢ Complete the form on the next page and detail all the monies you owe.

> ### EXECUTORS
>
> *Tell Us Once is a service which allows you to report a death to governmental organisations with one phone call. Once you have registered the death and have a reference number, you will be able to register for the service which will notify HMRC, Department of Work & Pensions, the Passport Office, DVLC, the local council and Veterans UK.*
>
> *Running in tandem with this is the Death Notification Service, a free service which, from a single interaction, multiple financial institutions can be contacted, reducing the number of calls and contacts that would otherwise be necessary. Details at the back of the book*

On the same page is a list of service providers. To what degree it needs to be completed is something only you can decide. However, it would useful for executors if you could highlight where there are agreements in place – such as a mobile phone, a car lease, entertainment and streaming contracts (Virgin Media, Sky, Netflix and so on), so the contract can be cancelled as soon as is practical.

When completing the form, also list advance subscriptions, such as membership fees of clubs and societies where a refund may be due.

LIABILITIES & LOANS	LOCATION OF PAPERWORK, POLICY NO.	OTHER INFORMATION
Bank loan		
Mortgage (1)		
Mortgage (2)		
Equity Release Plan		
Credit card (1)		
Credit card (2)		
Telephone		
Mobile Telephone		
TV/Broadband Provider		
Streaming Services		
Electric		
Gas		
Council Tax		
Water Rates		
Membership of club*		
Membership of club* (2)		

/   /   DATE

MONEY MATTERS | 59

1. For the sake of completeness, list all the property you own. Consider your home, as well as any holiday, investment and time-share property.

2. Where are the title deeds for each of these properties?

   (You may wish to use a blank page at the end of the book if there are a number.)

3. If you own your own home, are there any guarantees or permits which may be needed when selling it? (For example, planning consent, double glazed windows, conservatory, extensions etc.) Where can they be found?

> *Note: many people talk about "the deeds" to a property, but most details of property ownership are now held by (and are easily available from) the Land Registry.*
>
> *If you are unsure about the location of documents which show that you own the property, you can ask the solicitor who acted for you when you bought it. Alternatively, if you purchased the property with the help of a mortgage, the lender may know where the relevant documents are.*

4. If you have high-value assets, (such as your home, car, boat or caravan) which will need to be sold and form part of your estate, do you have any preference as to which agent is used to sell those assets? If you have valuation certificates or original receipts, where are these located?

5. Does anyone owe you any money? Is there any proof of this?

6. Do you wish your executors to try to recover this money and add it to your estate? If so, provide the contact details of the borrower:

7. Other than the items listed on the Liabilities and Loans form on Page 59, do you owe anyone money which will need to be paid out of your estate? Is there any proof of this? Where is the paperwork? List the contact details:

SECTION TEN

Taking Care of Business & Income Streams

According to the UK government, there were 5.6 million private sector businesses trading in the United Kingdom in 2023. Micro-businesses, with nought to nine employees, accounted for 5.4 million of those, but the overwhelming majority were the 4 million-plus sole traders.

In an ideal world, all business owners, regardless of the size of their concern, should have their business affairs in order; particularly if employees' livelihoods are at stake. Larger enterprises, such as limited companies and limited liability partnerships will probably have personnel who are aware of the workings of the company. Options for what action to take after an owner's death should be discussed with legal and financial advisors and beneficiaries to establish whether there is a willingness or the capability to take over the business as a going concern, or whether it should be wound up.

Perhaps more pertinent to the purpose of this book, are the 4.3 million sole traders: entrepreneurs, doing it for themselves. There are many strands to any individual business which are almost certainly unique. It stands to reason that for many such entrepreneurs, their business concerns are rarely shared with anyone other than, perhaps, the taxman. Going into extensive detail is beyond the scope of this book but, nonetheless, there are important practical issues which will need to be addressed. Even if your income stream from You-tube and social media platforms is modest, you should highlight them to enlighten your executors.

Consider putting together a file of your business concerns and ensure that your executors can access your computer and assist them further by including some of the basics on the following pages. If you have your fingers in several business pies, photocopy the forms in this section and complete a copy for each enterprise.

1. Do you own a business of any kind? State name, type and nature of it:

2. Confirm whether you are a sole trader, in a business partnership (LLP) or a limited company (Ltd)?

3. Where does your business operate from? Where are the keys for the premises? Is there an alarm?

4. If you rent any premises in connection with your business, who owns the building? Where is the lease contract?

5. Who knows about the day to day running of your business?

6. Does your business hold any trademarks or patents? Where is the paperwork?

7. If your business holds stock, where is it stored? Do your executors know how to access it?

8. Where can your executors find details on how to run your business?

    Consider your customer base, your suppliers, freelancers you may use and suchlike.

9.. Do you have any business vehicles? Are they leased or owned? Provide details:

10. Do you manage any websites? List the names and service providers of each.

    Ensure that your executors know how to access the service providers.

11. Do you have separate business email addresses (and therefore passwords)?

12. Do you have any online businesses? Consider online websites, eBay, Amazon and any other selling platforms. Give details of trading names used to sell.

13. If you use eBay, what name and email address is used to access your PayPal account(s)?

14. Do you have a YouTube Account from which you receive an income? Supply log in name and details.

15. Do you have any copyright material (images, photography, articles and so on) for which you receive an income? Consider online activity too.

16. Do you have any other source of income from online activities? Consider blogs and vlogs with advertising attached. What would you wish your executors to do with these?

    (Executors will have to familiarise themselves with the terms and conditions which were agreed to when you joined and may have no option but to close the account in accordance with those terms.)

17. Would you prefer for your business to continue trading or be sold? If the former, who should do this? Supply any other details that may assist:

BUSINESS	NAME/TITLE/NO	DETAILS
Company Name		
Company Unique Tax Ref.		
Tax Office		
Company House Registration No.		
Company House Log on Details		
VAT Registration No.		
Trademark(s)		
Location Of Payroll/Staff		
Assigned Business Telephone Number		
Business Insurance Policy		
Business Bank Account Sorting Code		
Accountant Details		
Email Address (1)		
Email Address (2)		
Twitter Account		
Business Facebook Page		
Business eBay Account		
Business PayPal Account		
Blog Details		
Dropbox account		

Additional Notes

So often it's the sentimental items on which no value can be placed which cause the most upset.

For me, the worst part of dealing with my grandad's estate was seeing his war medals and thus, legacy to society, given away without any consultation.

Roman Kubiak TEP,
Partner,
Head of Contested Wills Trusts and Estates at Hugh James, Cardiff.

The trouble is, often the problems arise not from the child of the deceased, but from the child's spouse……
the son's not bothered about the chattels – but his wife is!

Peter Hopkins TEP, Partner,
Mercers Solicitors,
Henley-on-Thames.

SECTION ELEVEN

Goods & Chattels

One of the most challenging and potentially stressful aspects for any executor to tackle is the distribution of the deceased's belongings. Whilst a Will advises of one's financial legacy in no uncertain terms, the absence of instructions on how to distribute possessions amplifies uncertainty in every shade of grey.

In an age of consumerism, we have more possessions than ever. Add to that the potential of a multi-faceted family unit, a second or third marriage or cohabitees with children and step-children, and one begins to grasp not just the complexities of individual family units but how the lines of ownership and claims for any single item of furniture, piece of jewellery or family heirloom could become confusing and ambiguous. Assessing but respecting the demands of a grieving family and a property full of possessions can prove to be a seriously challenging balancing act for even the most seasoned executor. Who is to receive Mum's cherished pearl necklace? Or Dad's stamp collection? If there is no surviving spouse or partner to assist or oversee proceedings or, if the deceased lived alone, without a Letter of Wishes to assist, it can be an overwhelming task for executors to uncover where, and to whom, any given item should go. So, there can be few more constructive and helpful tasks than assisting your executors now by pre-determining who should receive what.

Executors are not infallible, nor are they *Flog It* experts. An item of great value, which appears to be run-of-the-mill to the untrained eye, could end up being undersold or worse still, thrown away on the assumption that it's worthless tat. So, if you have valuable items, such as jewellery or works of art, they will need to be uncovered, identified and included in your estate. To avoid confusion or confrontation, you may wish to leave them to individuals in your Will. If you have a number of similar items – such as diamond rings, bracelets or artwork, take photographs or label them and verify to whom each one is left to avoid confusion. Alternatively, consider giving some of them away in the coming years. It is perfectly legal to give away up to £3,000 in cash or assets annually as part of your 'gift allowance'. It's another win-win: the item won't be subject to inheritance tax, you have the satisfaction of offering the item to your chosen beneficiary in person rather than after death.

Other belongings may not have great monetary value but could hold irreplaceable memories. Items which have been in the family for generations can be financially worthless but emotionally priceless. For those who are bereft, such pieces take on an importance which far outweighs their monetary value. If you have anything which could be considered a family heirloom in any shape or form (a trinket, medal, a first edition and so on), and your executors are unaware of its significance, make a note on one of following pages or at the back of this book detailing the history of the piece, its location and to whom it should be given. It does not matter how simple the item, the point is its relative sentimental value.

Bereavement is a difficult emotional process which can test any family's cohesion. Grief can produce feelings of anger, irritability and numbness which manifests as irrational and inconsiderate behaviour particularly when it comes to claiming chattels from the family home. Siblings who normally show each other respect suddenly morph into metaphorical tomb raiders while those paralyzed with grief, end up with crumbs; elder family members can assume authority while younger members hardly get a look in. Those living closest to the deceased's home invariably enjoy rich pickings while those who live further afield are left with remnants. Sadly, not only will these issues, paltry though they seem, stretch the bounds of what is legal, they are far from rare and can be the making of family feuds for years to come.

By completing details on the following pages, you can right some of these potential wrongs. Verify whether you have already promised (either in writing or in conversation) any item to any particular person. Claims made for the ownership of an item after someone's death are far from unusual, and, at a time of grief, families can fall out over the pettiest of issues, so it is in everyone's interest to have this section completed.

EXECUTORS

Choosing when and how to empty a property of belongings can be an extremely upsetting and should be dealt with great sensitivity. Whilst no one would wish the deceased's belongings to remain languishing in a property for years, nor would it be appropriate to empty it with unseeming haste unless circumstances dictate it to be necessary. Consider the bereaved, who may be struggling to come to terms with their loss.

Some religions believe the spirit of the deceased lives on within the property for days after death, so it may be respectful to bear that in mind if any mourners have spiritual leanings.

1. Your executors will need to secure your property by collecting all available keys. List everyone who has sets and their contact details:

2. Is your property alarmed? Who knows the code? Provide your executors with it. For security reasons, do not write it here.

3. Are there any other keys pertaining to your property – such as the back door key, a shed key, garage key? Where are they kept?

4. Does your property have a safe? If so, who is aware of its location and its code? If you have a partner or spouse, ensure they know how to access it. For security reasons, it is also advisable to pass this information on to your executors rather than writing it down here.

5. Do you have expensive assets (such as jewellery, works of art and so on) locked away with your bank or elsewhere for safekeeping? Ensure that your executors are aware of their existence and location. Where is the documentation to support this?

6. Does your property have a loft, cellar or cupboard which may not be obvious to your executors? Or do you have items in a storage facility in your building or elsewhere?
If so, where is it? How is it accessed?

7. Following your passing, there may be mourners and/or family members who wish to stay in your property. Is this acceptable to you, and does this relate to everyone, or only specific persons?

EXECUTORS

You are responsible for the deceased's possessions.

If you are aware of high value items or even items that could become the source of contention, remove them from the property for safe keeping.

Ideally, do this accompanied by a witness.

8. Other than your executors, who is to assist in emptying your home of your belongings? Has this been discussed and what, if any, provision has been made to enable this to happen?

9. What do you wish your executors to do with your clothes?

10. What do you wish your executors to do with your furniture?

11. If you are leaving specific items to individuals in your Will, are the executors aware of this?

12. Are there any items of any description within your home which belong to someone else?
    If so, what and to whom do they belong? Where can they be found?

➢ On the following page is a form to complete to state to whom you would wish to receive items.
➢ If you require more than one sheet, photocopy it and use the original as a template.

> Don't believe that appointing all of the children [as executors] will somehow cause unity, when ordinarily they don't get on – the added pressure and stress is likely to push them further apart.

Michelle Collins TEP, Partner,
Cozens-Hardy LLP,
Norwich.

ITEM DESCRIPTION	WHERE IS IT?	BEQUEATHED TO & CONTACT DETAILS?

Additional Notes

SECTION TWELVE

Children

Adequate provision should be made for children under the age of 18. With today's complicated lifestyle choices, this is clearly beyond the scope of this book; it must be dealt with in your Will, with the benefit of guidance from a competent solicitor, who may recommend trusts. Your solicitor will also, most likely, advise you to appoint guardians for worst case scenarios. Once guardians have been selected and agreed upon, you may wish to leave instructions on any preferences you have for your children regarding their education, religious upbringing, residence and so on. These guidelines will need to be reviewed from time to time, as your children mature and their circumstances change.

Particular attention should be given, and caution exercised, if you have a vulnerable child who may need specialist care into adulthood. In such cases, it is crucial that advice is sought from a solicitor who is fully conversant with not just the various trusts which are available, but also has an appreciation and experience as to the level of care your child may need. MENCAP has seen many cases where badly drafted Wills have had dire consequences for children.

If a suitable trust is not set up, a beneficiary can end up inheriting large sums of money which they may not have the capacity to deal with and which could, in turn, make them vulnerable to financial abuse. There is also the risk that a poorly considered legacy may affect their eligibility for future means-tested benefits. MENCAP provides a range of guidance literature and free telephone advice to parents and carers of anyone with a learning disability. The charity also holds a list of recommended solicitors who are fully conversant with both the financial and practical needs of the vulnerable.

For the sake of completeness, it is worth confirming a few details:

1. Write the names of your children and their dates and places of birth:

2. Supply the names of your children's guardians and their contact details:

   Guardian 1's Name: _____

   Address: _____

   Telephone numbers: _____

   Email address: _____

   Guardian 2's Name: _____

   Address: _____

   Telephone numbers: _____

   Email address: _____

3. What, if any, relation are the guardians to the children?

4. If your children are minors, where are their birth certificates kept?

5. Have you left any written instructions for the guardians of your children about your preferences in any of the topics raised earlier in this section (education, religious or health issues)? If so, where are they?

6. Are there any special requests with regard to your children which *have not* been mentioned in your Will which you wish to address now? Use the next page if necessary.

Additional Notes

SECTION THIRTEEN

Pooch, Puss & Pets

If you have a pet, the chances are that he or she means a great deal to you; in all likelihood, they are more than a companion, they are part of your family. It is important therefore that you make provision for their future welfare by finding them a new home. Whether that is simply discussing the issue with family members to ensure there is a willingness to take ownership or gifting the pet to a friend in your Will, it is advisable for all concerned to know ahead of time where the pet should go. You may also wish to leave some kind of additional financial bequest in your Will for your pet's care, stipulating that the funds are intended for its care to avoid confusion.

There are a number of options should no one wish to take on the role. Returning a pedigree to the breeder is an expensive option but there are two charities worthy of consideration. The RSPCA's Home for Life scheme will take care of the pet for the rest of its days or the Cinnamon Trust which, as well as homing an animal after the owner's death, will provide loving care for a pet should you be unable, for either temporary or permanent health reasons, to care for it during your lifetime. Both the RSPCA and the Cinnamon Trust require that a clause is inserted in your Will leaving the pet to the charity before they have the legal right to take ownership and subsequent care of the pet. See your solicitor or Will writer.

In any event, someone will need to familiarise themselves with the day-to-day care of your pet. Your input here will not only help the new owner but will also be hugely comforting for the grieving pet who has, after all, lost its owner and friend. It is likely to be confused and grieving, so completing this section will be very helpful for both. If you have more than one pet, complete this section using different coloured pens for each animal or assemble files and include relevant documentation.

1. What is your pet's name, breed and date of birth?

2. If your pet is a pedigree, do you have the documentation to support this? You may wish to include details of the breeder.

3. Do you have any vaccination certificates or micro-chip documentation for your pet? Where are they?

4. Which vet's practice (if any) do you use?

5. Has your pet, now or in the past, any significant medical conditions? Do you have pet insurance to cover the condition(s)?

6. Do you use a particular cattery or kennel for your pet? Supply details:

7. Is there anyone in particular you would like to look after him/her?
Have you discussed it with them? Supply their contact details.
Equally important, is there anyone you would rather did *not* take care of your pet?

8. Are there any special instructions which are needed for the care of the pet?

9. What type of food does your pet eat? Are there any special dietary requirements?

10. Do you have any other instructions which will assist your pet's carer?

    Consider your pet's likes and dislikes, favourite toys, habits…. anything that would help your pet's new carer.

Additional Notes

SECTION FOURTEEN

Last Orders

Having completed this book, you have done as much as you can do to ensure that your executors are equipped with the information they will need to carry out your *Last Orders*. As previously stated, the wishes laid out in this booklet are advisory, not mandatory.

If you have any last requests which involve your estate, you should ask your solicitor or Will-writer whether you need to alter your Will. It is advisable not to leave stray notes pertaining to finances, property or items of large monetary value with these *Last Orders* which are neither included in your Will nor a codicil, as it could cause significant ill feeling when they are discovered to be legally invalid.

Are there any issues which concern you which have not been covered in these pages?

Do you have any last requests that have not been addressed in this book?

Once you have completed your *Last Orders*, sign and date below to verify that the content represents your wishes. It is important that this is not witnessed, as it could invalidate your Will.

There are a number of blank pages overleaf where you can, if you wish, explain the reasoning - whether financial or emotional - behind your Will.

You may also wish to include any special thoughts you would like to share with your loved ones.

Signed   _____

Dated.   _____

Additional Notes

Additional Notes

Additional Notes

Additional Notes

USEFUL ADDRESSES

Celebration of Life
Enterprise House, Ocean Way, Southampton. SO14 3XB
Tel: 0800 150 3555
www.col.co.uk

Certainty Will Registry
The Chapel, Chapel Lane, Lapworth, Warwickshire, B94 6EU
Tel: 0845 408 0404
www.certainty.co.uk

Cinnamon Trust
10 Market Square, Hayle, Cornwall, TR27 4HE
Tel: 01736 757 900
www.cinnamon.org.uk

The Death Notification Service
www.deathnotificationservice.co.uk

Humanists UK
39 Moreland Street, London, EC1V 8BB
Tel: 020 7324 3060
www.humanism.org.uk

Human Tissue Authority (For Body Donation)
151 Buckingham Palace Road, Victoria, London, SW1W 9SZ
Tel: 020 7269 1999
www.hta.gov.uk

Institute of Civil Funerals
186a Station Road, Burton Latimer, Kettering, Northamptonshire, NN15 5NT
Tel: 01480 861411
www.iocf.org.uk

Institute of Professional Will Writers
Trinity Point, New Road, Halesowen, West Midlands, B63 3HY
Tel: 0345 257 2570
www.ipw.org.uk

The Law Society of England & Wales
The Law Society's Hall, 113 Chancery Lane, London WC2A 1PL
Tel: 020 7242 1222
www.lawsociety.org.uk

Legal Ombudsman
PO Box 6806, Wolverhampton, WV1 9WJ.
Tel: 0300 555 0333
www.legalombudsman.org.uk

Ministry of Justice (Lasting Power of Attorney Forms)
Tel: 0300 456 0300
www.justice.gov.uk/forms/opg/lasting-power-of-attorney

Ministry of Justice (Will storage)
Record Keeper's Department,
Principal Registry of the Family Division, First Avenue House,
42 - 49 High Holborn, London WC1V 6NP
Tel: 0300 123 1072
www.justice.gov.uk

My Lost Account (British Bankers' Association)
Lost Accounts Manager, The British Bankers' Association,
Pinners Hall, 105-108 Old Broad Street, London EC2N 1EX
www.mylostaccount.org.uk
Tel: 020 7216 8909

My Lost Account (Building Societies' Association)
Lost Savings, The Building Societies' Association,
6th Floor, York House, 23 Kingsway, London WC2B 6UJ
Tel: 020 7520 5900

My Lost Account (National Savings and Investments)
Tracing Service, National Savings and Investments,
Blackpool FY3 9YP
Tel: 0500 007 007

Organ Donation
NHS Blood and Transplant, Organ Donation & Transplantation Directorate,
Fox Den Road, Stoke Gifford, Bristol, BS34 8RR
Tel: 0300 123 2323
www.organdonation.nhs.uk

Royal Mencap Society,
123 Garden Lane, London, EC1Y 0RT
Tel: 020 7454 0454
www.mencap.org.uk

RSPCA Pet for Life
Wilberforce Way, Southwater, Horsham, West Sussex RH13 9RS
Tel: 0300 123 0239
www.homeforlife.org.uk

Society of Trust & Estate Practitioners (STEP)
Artillery House (South), 11 - 19 Artillery Row, London, SW1P 1RT
Tel: 020 7340 0500
www.step.org

Society of Will Writers
Newland House, Weaver Road, Lincoln, LN6 3QN.
Tel: 01522 687888
www.willwriters.com

Solicitors Regulation Authority,
The Cube, 199 Wharfside Street, Birmingham, B1 1RN
Tel: (0)121 329 6800
www.sra.org.uk

The Good Grief Trust (For Bereavement Support)
www.thegoodgrieftrust.org

Unclaimed Assets Register
The Sir John Peace Building, Experian Way, NG2 Business Park, Nottingham, NG80 1ZZ.
Tel: 0333 000 0182
www.uar.co.uk

ACKNOWLEDGEMENTS

In 2010, I went where none had ventured and published the first edition of *Last Orders* with little agenda other than to assist those who needed help to get their affairs in order. Little did I know that it would be embraced so wholly by professionals and the public that it would go on to reinvent my life.

It has been quite a journey of unanticipated surprises and unexpected joy. I am profoundly grateful for all the letters of thanks I have received from appreciative readers, countrywide. So, to all who have put pen to paper or sent an email, I thank you. Your kind words and affirmations have been heart-warming and motivated me to write this second edition.

I am indebted, too, to all who have helped spread the word that a Letter of Wishes is a vital part of getting one's affairs in order. To those who have, unbidden, taken the time to review *Last Orders* bringing it to the public's attention; to those who have, voluntarily, distributed the book's details on to friends and family and to the many professionals who have recommended and used it for their clients: to each and every one of you, a huge thank you.

For those professionals who are experts in their field and have generously allowed me to quote them in this edition: Michelle Collins, Peter Hopkins, Roman Kubiak and Gary Rycroft, I remain indebted.

Heartfelt thanks, too, must go to my legal advisor, Tim Bullimore, who is not just a marvellous sounding board but also a treasured friend.

Last but in no way least, I thank those who have been laid to rest. Without them I wouldn't have been able to write this book for you. They have each taught me well. So, I salute my friends Kate and Maria, my wonderful Mum and Dad and, more recently, dear Nigel Green, my delightful uncle Joe Martin and my cherished brother, Michael, who have all gone to their happy hunting ground much too soon. Thank you all.